Praise for BAPTIZING AMERICA

"A gang of White Nationalists crazies storm the U.S. Capitol, some of them carrying Christian crosses. See what you've done, all you right-wing, Evangelical preachers? You produced these wackos who can't tell the difference between the Kingdom of Heaven and the U.S.A. But now comes along Beau and Brian with a wallop of a book: well-researched, orthodox, fast-paced, and revealing. My own denomination's supposedly harmless, slightly to the left, "God Bless America" sentimentality is revealed to be a precursor of a mess like January 6. This book has caused this mainliner to take a sober theological assessment of my church and its unknowing complicity in the naissance of ugly Christian Nationalism. Thanks to *Baptizing America*, I have met the syncretistic, idolatrous, confused Nationalist. It turns out that he looks like the nice, middle-of-the-road, moderate, Methodist me. Oops."

— Rev. Will Willimon, United Methodist Bishop (retired), Professor of the Practice of Christian Ministry, Duke Divinity School, and author of *Accidental Preacher: A Memoir*.

"Kaylor and Underwood provide a compelling narrative regarding the role of mainline Protestantism in establishing Christian Nationalism as part of the mainstream of American civic life. Understanding this history clarifies the current context and signals where we go from here. Anyone interested in confronting and opposing Christian Nationalism must read this book."

— Dr. Andrew Whitehead, Associate Professor of Sociology at Indiana University-Indianapolis and author of *American Idolatry: How Christian Nationalism Betrays the Gospel and Threatens the Church*.

"Like so many other -isms, mainline churches need to interrogate their own complicity in the rise and perpetuation of Christian Nationalism. Being aware of how our language and actions create problematic conflations between Christianity and any form of nationalism requires constant vigilance. Brian Kaylor and Beau Underwood have written a candid word to mainliners that arises from their appreciation for this tradition. I hope we will learn from this book and allow it to shape our future witness to the God who is above all nations."

— Rev. Teresa "Terri" Hord Owens, General Minister and President, Christian Church (Disciples of Christ) in the U.S. and Canada.

"I have come to count on Kaylor and Underwood for their thorough and detailed historical context to understand how Christian Nationalism is spreading in harmful ways today. Their new book adds an important and provocative angle for Christians from the mainline Protestant denominations to examine their own complicity with perpetuating Christian Nationalism and White supremacy. Kaylor and Underwood helpfully add to the conversation by showing how Christian Nationalism flourishes in Christian circles outside of White evangelicalism."

— Amanda Tyler, executive director of Baptist Joint Committee for Religious Liberty, lead organizer of Christians Against Christian Nationalism, and author of the forthcoming *How to End Christian Nationalism.*

"With deep historical research and trenchant analysis, Brian Kaylor and Beau Underwood have produced a jeremiad that expands the net of complicity for Christian Nationalism beyond the usual suspects. *Baptizing America* is an important book that exposes both the roots and the effects of this cancer while offering suggestions on how to fight it."

— Dr. Randall Balmer, John Phillips Professor in Religion at Dartmouth College, Episcopal priest, and author of *Saving Faith: How American Christianity Can Reclaim Its Prophetic Voice.*

"Kaylor and Underwood's *Baptizing America* is an essential contribution to the growing body of work on Christian Nationalism in the United States. Christian Nationalism is a grave threat to American democracy. Many clergy, scholars, and journalists have written about the ways it threatens our nation and the Christian church by focusing on evangelical and charismatic movements and communities. But no other work so persuasively and daringly articulates how mainline Christians have cultivated Christian Nationalism in ways that harm the American public square. It is thorough and detailed in its analysis; unflinching in its conclusions. This book is required reading for anyone who wants to face the hard truth that Christian Nationalism is a mainline issue that must be addressed in order to create a more perfect union for all."

— Dr. Bradley Onishi, Research Associate at the UC Berkeley Center for the Study of Religion, co-host of *Straight White American Jesus* podcast, and author of *Preparing for War: The Extremist History of White Christian Nationalism—And What Comes Next.*

"White Christianity is a heresy. So is American Christianity. Christianity should always be the first word for us who are followers of Jesus. We are Christians first. This book shows how all of White Christianity, including mainline Protestants, has fallen victim to American nationalism. But it also suggests how mainline Protestants could help us find a better way, not just by blaming others, but leading by example."

— Rev. Jim Wallis, Archbishop Desmond Tutu Chair in Faith and Justice and Director of the Center on Faith and Justice at Georgetown University, founder of Sojourners, and author of *The False White Gospel: Rejecting Christian Nationalism, Reclaiming True Faith, and Refounding Democracy.*

"*Baptizing America* is a critical resource for ministers, policymakers, and advocates seeking to root out the idolatry of Christian Nationalism now threatening democracies globally. Its authors convinced me it is too simplistic to point the finger at White evangelicals. We mainline Protestants must interrogate our own history and consider how our hymns, creeds, symbols, notions of civic religion, and political missteps have primed our people to be all too receptive to a Christianity weaponized for political purposes. I emerged from its pages with new questions, helpful strategies, and renewed purpose for transformational ministry in this critical era of church and democratic decline."

— Rev. Jennifer Butler, Executive Director of Faith in Democracy, founder and former CEO of Faith in Public Life, Presbyterian minister, and author of *Who Stole My Bible: Reclaiming Scripture as a Handbook for Resisting Tyranny.*

"A deeply faithful and patriotic book, *Baptizing America* shines a spotlight on the unacknowledged role mainline Protestantism played in creating modern-day Christian Nationalism. Equally important, the book offers a roadmap for how mainline Protestants today can exorcise Christian Nationalism from their own faith tradition which, in my opinion, will make for better religion and a healthier democracy."

— Rev. Paul Brandeis Raushenbush, President & CEO of the Interfaith Alliance and American Baptist minister.

"*Baptizing America* offers a stringent critique not just of contemporary reactionary right-wing Christian Nationalism but all forms of U.S. civil religion, including that found historically and in current mainline/liberal Protestantism. The authors' challenge is offered for the sake both of the church's spiritual integrity and the state's constitutional and democratic order. This is a book that sharpens to a very fine edge the argument about the relationship between Christianity and public life in America."

— Dr. David P. Gushee, Distinguished University Professor of Christian Ethics at Mercer University, Chair of Christian Social Ethics at *Vrije Universiteit* ("Free University") Amsterdam/IBTS, and author of *Defending Democracy From Its Christian Enemies.*

BAPTIZING AMERICA

How Mainline Protestants Helped Build Christian Nationalism

Brian Kaylor & Beau Underwood

Foreword by Adriene Thorne
Senior Minister of The Riverside Church

chalice
PRESS

Copyright ©2024 Brian Kaylor & Beau Underwood

All rights reserved. For permission to reuse content, please contact Copyright Clearance Center, 222 Rosewood Drive, Danvers, MA 01923, (978) 750-8400, www.copyright.com.

Print: 9780827203389

EPUB: 9780827203396

EPDF: 9780827203402

ChalicePress.com

Printed in the United States of America

Dedicated to all our fellow Christians

who still advocate for the separation of church and state.

The group discussion guide for *Baptizing America* is available as a free download:

wordandway.org/baptizingamerica

ChalicePress.com

TABLE OF CONTENTS

FOREWORD

"Don't let anybody make you think that God chose America as his divine messianic force to be a sort of policeman of the whole world. God has a way of standing before the nations with justice and it seems that I can hear God saying to America, 'You are too arrogant. If you don't change your ways, I will rise up and break the backbone of your power, and I will place it in the hands of a nation that doesn't even know my name.'"

—*Rev. Dr. Martin Luther King, Jr.*

Oof! Brian Kaylor and Beau Underwood's book landed like a rock in my inbox and spirit, but it has proven to be just the heavy lift I aspire to hoist as I lament the religious and political fabric of the United States of America pulling apart and weakening daily. The authors starkly reveal for mainline Protestants what the 1979 horror film reminded us, "The call is coming from inside the house." They assemble stories and records that make evident the ways mainliners created the very ideology we detest. Mixing faith identity and national identity, we produced the intoxicating cocktail now known as Christian Nationalism. The authors have the receipts to prove the claim.

Perhaps you read the title of this fine book multiple times and asked yourself how the publishers allowed the manuscript to go to print with such a glaring typographical error. The answer is they did not. Despite the fact that mainline Protestant churches, and others, associate Christian Nationalism today with evangelical, right-leaning communities of faith, the truth is that my progressive siblings and I play(ed) a part in building and maintaining the very destructive beliefs that we abhor ... except, of course, when we are invoking them. We take great delight in pointing fingers at the other side—perhaps because our version is a softer, gentler form of nationalism—but nonetheless, in our worship, our silence, and our proximity to political power we too often invoke divine blessings on our "one nation under God."

Now, before you throw your hands up in despair or begin to self-defend, as I did many times while reading, take a deep breath. Prepare yourself instead for a well-researched and often cheeky romp through American history. Prepare to understand our nation's story through the stained-glass windows of the Christian church. Prepare to have your socks blown off reading stories of Christian leaders and politicians walking proverbially hand in hand—stories I guarantee you have never heard. The authors perform an impressive, convincing, and surprisingly humorous indictment of mainline Protestants that invite us to some good old-fashioned truth-telling and confession, for those inclined to such activities. I hope you are. Changing the nationalistic recipe that mainline faith leaders helped concoct will depend on our willingness to admit where we went wrong. It will also require our commitment to do better.

Because I can already hear the knuckles cracking from the handwringing and the plaintive cries about what to do, know that the book concludes with many theologically grounded actions that you can employ to combat Christian Nationalism in yourself and in your community of faith. The authors have not left us bereft of ways to protect democracy or, most importantly, to combat the weaponization of Christian faith, to lift up the global gospel of Jesus Christ, and to love our neighbors as ourselves ... regardless of how they name God or if they name God at all. Reminder: that is part of the beauty of living in a democratic nation.

This literary offering is a necessary blow to the body of Christ, in that it is an invitation to course correct. Reading forces us to pause and notice the ways that we entwine the cross with the flag, and bids us to take repentant action. I believe God's people are often doing the best we can. Sometimes we act out of fear and sometimes we are able to muster our God-given gifts and act out of love. We are not exceptional, but we can act exceptionally and collaboratively with great love.

The time is always right for a U-turn in the way we understand, name, and engage Christian Nationalism. I hope, dear reader, that you will make a U-turn with me. I hope you will read the book, share the book, and study the book. Most importantly for our churches and our nation, I pray you will take a U-turn and engage the actions the authors suggest.

I cannot say how I came to believe that God loved all the children of God. I do not remember anyone teaching me that all the children included other faiths as well as those who did not name God at all, but God's love for all of God's people is one truth I know for sure. Christian Nationalism is not Christian and it is not democratic. Thank you for using your platform and your connections to ensure religious freedom and democracy for all the people … regardless. Thank you for acting, to the extent you are able, from love rather than fear. May God bless all the people and all the good creation.

Rev. Adriene Thorne
Senior Minister, The Riverside Church in the City of New York
December 2023

Section I

CHRISTIAN NATIONALISM
IN CONTEXT

Chapter 1

HOW FIRM A FOUNDATION

A preacher stood on the steps of the U.S. Capitol on January 6 and prayed aloud for America to be "one nation under God." Those nearby him sang Christian hymns as they suggested God supported them against their political opponents. But this wasn't during the insurrection of 2021. This scene emerged one year later as Rev. Michael Curry, presiding bishop of the Episcopal Church, prayed during a remembrance service hosted by congressional Democrats.

A year earlier, a pro-Trump mob had demonstrated the threat of Christian Nationalism as people violently stormed the Capitol while carrying Christian flags, Bibles, and signs professing their faith in Jesus. Many offered prayers as they entered—and damaged—the temple of American democracy. Christian Nationalism helped fuel the deadly events of that day, rightly leading many scholars, journalists, and clergy to condemn the ideology as dangerous and heretical. But after the smoke cleared, the certification of President Joe Biden's win occurred, and workers cleaned up the trash and human excrement, a distorted picture emerged that depicted Christian Nationalism as an aberration unique to right-wing evangelicals.

If January 6, 2021, showed us the depth of Christian Nationalism among conservative evangelicals and Pentecostals, then January 6, 2022, proved revelatory in its own way. The first anniversary highlighted the breadth of this ideology across our political and theological continuums. Addressing the threat of Christian Nationalism requires an honest acknowledgment of all the places it shows up and the historical forces that contributed to its rise.

After a day of reflecting on the insurrection a year earlier and emphasizing the importance of upholding democracy, congressional Democrats gathered on the steps of the east entrance to the Capitol. These are the same stairs where members of both parties crowded together on September 11, 2001, to sing "God Bless America" on the evening of the deadly attacks in Washington, D.C., and New York City. Two decades later, the spirit of bipartisanship was gone. But Democrats returned to that same place to reassure the nation that God still favored the American government.

Although most of the pro-Trump mob 365 days earlier had arrived on the other side of the Capitol that faces the Washington Monument, some had also pushed through barricades on this side. Instead of Trump, yellow Gadsden snake, and "An Appeal to Heaven" flags waving on those steps as they had a year before, the congressional members carried candles. Dozens of other candles lit up the stairs, giving the moment a solemn, worshipful ambiance.

The brief eight-minute service that followed lacked any pretense of an interfaith gathering.[1] Instead, it was a prayer vigil that could have comfortably occurred inside a church. And the service embodied Christian Nationalism rather than challenging the ideology that inspired many who stood on those steps a year earlier.

Curry kicked off the gathering with prayer. Quoting from the New Testament, he declared that God is love. He also praised God as "the fountain of all wisdom and the light of all truth." He prayed that the elected lawmakers present behind him would be God's "instruments" to bring peace, love, and healing. And he invoked God's blessing on America in Christian Nationalistic terms.

"We need your help, Lord, now, to be the democracy you would have us to be, to be the nation you would have us to be—one nation under God, indivisible, with liberty and justice for all," he prayed.

Following Curry's prayer, Master Sergeant Sara Sheffield of "the President's own United States Marine Band" (as she was introduced) sang "My Country, 'Tis of Thee." In addition to the famous first verse,

---

[1] "Congressional Leaders Hold Vigil on January 6 Anniversary," C-SPAN, January 6, 2022, https://www.c-span.org/video/?517013-1/ congressional-vigil-january-6-anniversary.

the only other stanza she sang was the fourth—the most Christian Nationalistic of the verses:

Our fathers' God, to thee,
Author of liberty,
To thee we sing;
Long may our land be bright
With freedom's holy light;
Protect us by thy might,
Great God our king!

Speaker of the House Nancy Pelosi led a moment of silence "in memory of those who lost their lives and sacrificed so much for our democracy that day." After that, Sheffield sang "God Bless America," which some members of Congress joined in singing. Then the vigil suddenly ended. The whole service had included nothing more than two hymns from the Christian Nationalism hymnbook, a prayer from a Christian minister blessing the country as "one nation under God," and a moment of silence led by a Christian politician.

If that service had been exactly the same but we switched out the leaders with conservative evangelical figures, it would have quickly been criticized by many as Christian Nationalism. Imagine Paula White-Cain saying the prayer, Sean Feucht singing those hymns, and Speaker Mike Johnson introducing the moment of silence. But those individuals were not part of an official government service on the steps of the Capitol on January 6, 2022. It turns out that Christian Nationalism doesn't show up at the Capitol only during an insurrection.

Yet, despite many scholars, journalists, and religious leaders documenting the role Christian Nationalism played in the events of January 6, 2021, the official response a year later was just to try a softer, cuddlier version of the ideology. It was almost like our nation's leaders weren't paying attention to what had actually occurred a year earlier.

Rachel Laser, president and CEO of Americans United for Separation of Church and State,[2] argued in response to the vigil that "whenever the government sponsors an official prayer vigil,

---

[2] In full disclosure, one of us (Brian) serves on the board of trustees for Americans United for Separation of Church and State.

it sends the message that some of us belong more than others."[3] But she found it particularly problematic on the anniversary of the January 6 insurrection:

> When the government sponsors the prayer vigil as a way to commemorate a Christian Nationalist attack on the U.S. Capitol, it is especially insulting to our foundational principle of religious freedom. Instead, the government should use the occasion to remind people that it is the secular nature of our government that fortifies our democracy and frees us to come together as equals.

It's true that the Christian Nationalism on display on January 6, 2022, didn't spark a violent attack on police officers or literally leave a mark on the walls and windows of the Capitol. But that doesn't render it harmless. No matter who expresses it, Christian Nationalism does violence to our nation's pluralistic ideals and the teachings of Jesus. And while many are quick to castigate extreme right-wing religious and political leaders for endorsing its ideas, they were not the ones who prepared the way for the influence it holds in our contemporary public life.

Defining the Problem

As attention to Christian Nationalism rises, the concept ironically becomes more ambiguous. Different people employ the term in various ways that cause one to consider whether they are all talking about the same thing. This is especially problematic as some right-wing politicians and preachers now embrace the label while also trying to give it a positive spin.[4] Definitions are important here because effectively grasping and responding to the problem requires some precision in understanding what Christian Nationalism is and is not.

Sociologists Andrew Whitehead and Samuel Perry, two of the most authoritative voices on Christian Nationalism in the United States, define it as "a cultural framework—a collection of myths, traditions, symbols, narratives, and value systems—that idealizes

---

[3] Brian Kaylor and Beau Underwood, "The Prayers of January 6," *A Public Witness*, January 6, 2022, https://publicwitness.wordandway.org/p/the-prayers-of-january-6.

[4] Brian Kaylor and Beau Underwood, "Badge of Honor," *A Public Witness*, July 21, 2022, https://publicwitness.wordandway.org/p/badge-of-honor.

and advocates a fusion of Christianity with American civic life."[5] In other words, Christian Nationalism seeks to conflate national and religious identities in a way that inherently provides Christians with a privileged place in American society. The "Christians Against Christian Nationalism" movement spearheaded by the Baptist Joint Committee for Religious Liberty unpacks the idea as this: "Christian Nationalism seeks to merge Christian and American identities, distorting both the Christian faith and America's constitutional democracy. Christian Nationalism demands Christianity be privileged by the State and implies that to be a good American, one must be Christian."[6] Christian Nationalism tries to accomplish this by narrowly defining who counts as Christian and retelling the story of America in ways that promote a particular hierarchy. Christian Nationalism seeks a social order where Christians control the levers of power and others assume subservient roles within this so-called "Christian nation."[7]

Yet, some insist the ideology isn't real. Franklin Graham, the controversial son of the famed evangelist Billy Graham, declared in 2021 that "Christian Nationalism doesn't exist."[8] He added, "It's just another name to throw at Christians." Such claims attempt to defuse critiques of those propagating the ideology by arguing the term is ambiguous, subjective, or leveraged by one group to make their opponents look bad. While cable news provides bountiful evidence of our political polarization, Christian Nationalism is not a weapon in our partisan wars. Instead, it is a phenomenon carefully studied and measured by social scientists.

A common approach by Whitehead, Perry, and others is to use large surveys where respondents express their opinions on issues

---

[5] Andrew Whitehead and Samuel Perry, *Taking America Back for God: Christian Nationalism in the United States*, (New York: Oxford University Press, 2022), 10.

[6] "Christians Against Christian Nationalism," Christians Against Christian Nationalism, https://www.christiansagainstchristiannationalism.org/statement.

[7] For a detailed explanation, see Philip Gorski and Samuel Perry, *The Flag & The Cross: White Christian Nationalism and the Threat to American Democracy* (New York: Oxford University Press, 2022).

[8] Eliza Griswold, "A Pennsylvania Lawmaker and the Resurgence of Christian Nationalism," *The New Yorker*, May 9, 2021, https://www.newyorker.com/news/on-religion/a-pennsylvania-lawmaker-and-the-resurgence-of-christian-nationalism.

related to religion in public life. Scholars then combine responses to various questions to create a scale expressing the intensity (or lack thereof) of support for Christian Nationalism. Here's the key thing: using common statistical tools, these researchers demonstrate that how one scores on the Christian Nationalism scale relate to one's views on a host of other political and social issues. These statistical techniques also allow scholars to control for other factors, rendering them confident that a significant relationship exists between Christian Nationalism and these various subjects. Contrary to Graham's protestations, Christian Nationalism is a very real thing that is connected to other aspects of our common life. And as the scholarship shows, it's a powerful ideology that impacts what people believe about a host of religious, political, and cultural issues. A deep dive into the social science is beyond the purview of this book, but the research is there for anyone with access to the Internet and the time to digest it.

We should make one additional comment here. The term "Christian Nationalism" is relatively new in our public discourse, but the idea has a long history. Phrases like "civil religion," "American exceptionalism," "religious nationalism," and others contain elements of what is now labeled as Christian Nationalism. The argument in this book uses the lens of Christian Nationalism to comprehend and interrogate past events that made the ideology's present intensity possible. The label may be anachronistic but the aptness of the application is not. Indeed, our main point is that we should be consistent in what we name as Christian Nationalism regardless of when it arises and who promotes it.

Another term requiring definition is "mainline Protestant." The label attempts to carve out a particular group of Christians for understanding and analysis, but who exactly falls under its banner and what they supposedly have in common is not always clear. Mainline is not shorthand for "progressive Christian." Many mainliners would not define themselves with that label. Many others would describe themselves as theologically progressive but are not typically understood to be part of the mainline tradition. Political scientist and American Baptist pastor Ryan Burge has noted that social scientists studying religion typically categorize people according to either belief (the views they hold), behavior (the practices they perform), or belonging (the groups they participate in). As a category, mainline Protestants are most easily understood in terms of their denominational belonging.[9]

A common definition of mainline Protestants focuses on the historic denominations sometimes called the "Seven Sisters": American Baptist Churches USA, Christian Church (Disciples of Christ), Episcopal Church, Evangelical Lutheran Church in America, Presbyterian Church (U.S.A.), United Church of Christ, and United Methodist Church. At different points and places, these denominations enjoyed significant cultural cachet, but declining membership and broader societal changes have reduced their influence.[10] Given their prominence and size, these faith groups pop up most frequently in our analysis of how mainline Protestants helped create Christian Nationalism. They produced more leaders in Washington, D.C., led the ecumenical movement, and enjoyed more cultural influence during the events we cover.

"Mainline Protestant denominations have played an outsized role in America's history, given that most of the nation's founders were members of what we now refer to as mainline Protestant churches. Until the 1960s, more than half of American adults identified with the largest seven mainline Protestant traditions," PRRI explained in a 2023 study on mainline clergy.[11]

However, the term "mainline" today is often much broader in use to include similarly-minded Protestant groups outside the larger "Seven Sisters." In fact, PRRI in its polling breaks down White Christianity into three categories: White Catholic, White evangelical Protestant, and "White mainline (non-evangelical) Protestant." They often separate out Black and Hispanic Catholics and Protestants because they hold different religious and political

---

[9] Ryan Burge, *The Nones: Where They Came From, Who They Are, and Where They Are Going* (Minneapolis: Fortress Press, 2023), 8–17.

[10] For a fuller discussion on these dynamics, see Jason Lanzer, *Mainline Christianity: The Past and Future of America's Majority Faith* (New York: NYU Press, 2012).

[11] "Clergy and Congregations in a Time of Transformation: Findings from the 2022-2023 Mainline Protestant Clergy Survey," PRRI, Sept. 13, 2023, https://www.prri.org/research/clergy-and-congregations-in-a-time-of-transformation-findings-from-the-2022-2023-mainline-protestant-clergy-survey.

views from their co-religionists. But viewing Protestants as either evangelical or mainline is a helpful dichotomy. While perhaps not a perfect definition by essentially dividing Protestants into just two camps, it still captures significant differences within American Protestantism that explain much of our divides on religious and political issues.

Pew Research Center similarly divides White Protestants into either evangelical or mainline categories.[12] They have even classified various denominations, which not only provides a helpful list but also shows how the evangelical-mainline split runs through traditions. For instance, among Baptists they include the Southern Baptist Convention and numerous smaller groups in the evangelical category, while coding two denominations as mainline: American Baptists and the Cooperative Baptist Fellowship. Similarly, among Presbyterians one can find mainliners in the Presbyterian Church (U.S.A.) or evangelicals in the Presbyterian Church in America and some smaller groups. Lutherans also show how labels can get messy as the largest group, Evangelical Lutheran Church in America, is mainline despite having "evangelical" in its name while the next largest group, Lutheran Church–Missouri Synod, is evangelical. Some other mainline denominations not in the "Seven Sisters" include Church of the Brethren, Mennonite Church USA, Metropolitan Community Churches, and Moravian Church in America.

Together, mainline Protestants still represent a significant religious tradition in the U.S., even if their glory days of cultural dominance have passed. So while much ink has been spilled since the Capitol insurrection about evangelicals and Christian Nationalism, we turn to the other half of White Protestantism. Although evangelicals had been the larger group in recent years after mainline decline in the latter half of the twentieth century, evangelicals are now also experiencing decline. PRRI found in 2022 that 13.6% of the U.S. population was White evangelical while 13.9% were White mainline Protestant. Only the "religiously unaffiliated"

---

[12] "The Digital Pulpit: A Nationwide Analysis of Online Sermons," Pew Research Center, December 16, 2019, 40–45, https://www.pewresearch. org/religion/wp-content/uploads/sites/7/2019/12/PF.12.16.19_ sermons.analysis.appendix.pdf.

category included a higher percentage of Americans (26.8%) than those two groups.[13]

While mainline Protestants are not as numerous as they once were, it's important to grasp at the outset how their past dominance shaped the present in important ways. For example, historian David Hollinger argued that reactions against the decisions and articulations of mainline Protestants drove and defined the growth of the mid-twentieth century evangelicalism, including that movement's conservative political engagement. In tracing those developments, he also articulated a helpful nuance for distinguishing mainline Protestants from other U.S. Christians. These churches can be historically distinguished by their embrace of (rather than opposition to) many Enlightenment ideas and an ecumenical disposition seen in their "willingness to cooperate in ecclesiastical, civic, and global affairs with a great variety of groups that professed to be Christian, and many that did not."[14] While our argument emphasizes the past actions of those who belonged to mainline Protestant churches, it also highlights the beliefs expressed by that group of Christians. The tendency of mainliners to see themselves as collaborating with others to steward not only their specific faith traditions but also the broader culture created an environment where God and country were too easily joined together. The relationship was perceived as mutually edifying—or at least innocuous—but has proven to be destructive to both.

Christian writer and historian Diana Butler Bass succinctly stated that the term "mainline" is "a sociological/historically assigned category that aptly described [mainliners] position vis-a-vis culture, politics of the mid-late twentieth century."[15] Our contention is that the cultural and political preeminence mainliners possessed in this era and after inadvertently became the seedbed out of which much of today's Christian Nationalism grew. Effectively

[13] "PRRI 2022 Census of American Religion: Religious Affiliation Updates and Trends," PRRI, February 24, 2023, https://www.prri.org/spotlight/prri-2022-american-values-atlas-religious-affiliation-updates-and-trends.

[14] David Hollinger, *Christianity's American Fate: How Religion Became More Conservative and Society More Secular* (Princeton: Princeton University Press, 2022), 3.

[15] Diana Butler Bass (@dianabutlerbass), Twitter, June 26, 2023, https://twitter.com/dianabutlerbass/status/1673403803620757504.

addressing this problem requires an honest assessment of these roots that give it life.

A False Diagnosis

Christian Nationalism was an ideology and a term in use in scholarship and public discourse before the Capitol insurrection. Despite that, many people fail to connect the dots. Such short-sightedness can lead to a belief that simply removing Donald Trump from public life would completely heal our politics. Congressional Democrats—and the few Republicans who spoke out against the Trump-led insurrection—demonstrated this blindspot about Christian Nationalism with the release of the December 2022 report from the House Select Committee that investigated the attack on the Capitol. During high-profile public hearings leading up to the report's release, the committee spent time highlighting how Trump told supporters he would march with them and even argued with his staff who successfully prevented that from occurring. While Trump didn't march to the Capitol, Christian Nationalism did. But none of the hearings covered the ideology that inspired many who did storm the Capitol, attack police officers, threaten congressional members, and try to overturn a free and fair election.

The silence about Christian Nationalism in the hearings came even after several leaders of Christian denominations urged the committee to "focus questioning and discussion on Christian Nationalism and the role it played in bolstering, justifying, and intensifying the January 6 attack."[16] The faith leaders explained that as Christians they "are deeply concerned about Christian Nationalism and its danger not only to our constitutional democracy but in its distortion of Christianity."[17] Their pleas went unheeded and their prayers unanswered.

After 17 months of investigations, hundreds of interviews, several successful court battles to get documents, and nearly a dozen public hearings, the House Select Committee released its

---

[16] Jack Jenkins and Emily McFarlan Miller, "Major Christian Leaders Asked Jan. 6 Committee to Investigate Christian Nationalism," *Religion News Service*, November 3, 2022, https://religionnews.com/2022/11/03/major-christian-leaders-asked-jan-6-committee-to-investigate-christian-nationalism.

[17] Jenkins and Miller," Jan. 6 Committee."

845-page final report. But don't bother flipping through it to find the documentation or discussion on Christian Nationalism's role in fueling the insurrection—because the committee virtually ignored the topic. The report names Christian Nationalism only once: as it describes the movement led by the far-right provocateur Nick Fuentes (who also sparked controversy in 2022 for dining with Trump and the rapper Ye because of Fuentes and Ye's record of antisemitic and other extremist views). The report notes in passing that Fuentes and his followers "have repeatedly promoted White supremacist and Christian Nationalist beliefs."[18] Bizarrely, there are as many instances of "Islamic terrorism" in the report as instances of Christian Nationalism. There's another reference to "the self-proclaimed 'Judeo-Christian' Jericho March organization," and three citations in the footnotes to a *Washington Post* article by Peter Manseau about the religious influences on one insurrectionist. And those are *all* the times "Christian" shows up (not counting one reference to a person's name).

Other religious terms don't show up in the report much either. There are just a few references to "God" or "prayer," and none to "Bible" or "crucifix" despite insurrectionists carrying such symbols along with the Christian flag (a detail also not mentioned in the report even though Confederate, Trump, and QAnon flags are highlighted). And there's just one occurrence of "Jesus," but it was uttered by someone who was attacked by MAGA backers because of Trump's lies about the election. Reading the report, one would almost think religion had nothing to do with January 6. But, unfortunately and obviously, it did.

The virtual silence by the House Select Committee on Christian Nationalism was a calculated political choice. This move was guided particularly by the committee's vice chair, Rep. Liz Cheney. Accounts emerged shortly before the report's release that she wanted the final product to focus on Trump and to avoid other conclusions that could be alienating. As her spokesperson told the *Washington Post*, "She won't sign onto any 'narrative' that suggests Republicans are inherently racist, or smears men and women in law enforcement, or

---

[18] *Final Report: Select Committee to Investigate the January 6th Attack on the United States Capitol*, December 22, 2022, https://www.govinfo.gov/content/pkg/GPO-J6-REPORT/pdf/GPO-J6-REPORT.pdf.

suggests every American who believes God has blessed America is a White supremacist."[19] Cheney sacrificed her own political career to put the nation ahead of her party's leader. She thus deserves praise as a rare, principled politician. But she's wrong on this point. And the caricature offered by her spokesman is unhelpful. Talking about the demonstrable role Christian Nationalism played in the insurrection, which has been well documented by journalists and scholars, is not tantamount to depicting any God-loving person as a White supremacist. By refusing to acknowledge (or perhaps even understand) Christian Nationalism, Cheney and her spokesperson led the committee to miss an important reason the insurrection even happened.

Rev. Nathan Empsall, executive director of Faithful America, noted the problem with the committee's report:

> The January 6 Committee giving only passing mention to the pivotal role of Christian Nationalism in its final report is a missed opportunity to fully understand what led to the violence at the Capitol—and to prevent future political violence. It is undeniable that Christian Nationalism played a key role in the January 6 insurrection, when Donald Trump and his corrupt allies warped and abused Christian imagery to justify their violent, hate-fueled power grab.[20]

Simply removing Trump from the political landscape won't fix the problem. Because Christian Nationalism predates him and even the political rise of his evangelical base.

Yet, rather than recognizing the role Christian Nationalism played in the lead-up to the insurrection, Cheney instead seemed to think the antidote to Trump was just a kinder version of Christian Nationalism. Cheney, a United Methodist, pushed the narrative of the U.S. as a Christian nation during the committee's hearings. Specifically, she insisted that "our Constitution is indeed a divinely inspired document" as she emphasized the importance

---

[19] Jacqueline Alemany, Josh Dawsey, and Carol D. Leonnig, "Jan. 6 Panel Staffers Angry at Cheney for Focusing So Much of Report on Trump," *Washington Post*, November 23, 2022, https://www.washingtonpost.com/politics/2022/11/23/liz-cheney-jan-6-committee.

[20] Brian Kaylor and Beau Underwood, "The Missing Pages in the Jan. 6 Report," *A Public Witness*, Dec. 26, 2022, https://publicwitness.wordandway.org/p/the-missing-pages-in-the-jan-6-report.

of remembering "what it means to take an oath under God to the Constitution."[21] We shouldn't be surprised to see Cheney steered the focus away from Christian Nationalism as she embraced the idea of the U.S. being a "Christian" nation. After all, before the insurrection she defended a privileged place for God in government and even weaponized faith against her political opponents.

In January 2019, House Democrats considered removing "so help me God" from the end of oaths administered to witnesses swearing to tell the truth. Although often said, the phrase is generally not included in the official, required language. For instance, presidents today utter that phrase even though it's not in the oath spelled out word-for-word in the Constitution and none likely used it before Chester Arthur in 1881.[22] Nonetheless, the move by Democrats— even though some Republicans had omitted the phrase in previous hearings—sparked headlines on Fox News and conservative Christian websites. Cheney quickly took the bait.

"It is incredible, but not surprising, that the Democrats would try to remove God from committee proceedings in one of their first acts in the majority," she argued. "They really have become the party of Karl Marx."[23]

After Rep. Jared Huffman, a California Democrat who was the only member of Congress who identified as a humanist, criticized Cheney's comments, Cheney's spokesperson shot back: "Liz Cheney will always defend God. Period. If that bothers Rep. Huffman, we'll be praying for him."[24]

While we believe in praying for people, the tone didn't actually sound sincere. We're also not sure how it makes sense to demand

---

[21] "Here's Every Word from the Fourth Jan. 6 Committee Hearing on Its Investigation," NPR, June 21, 2022, https://www.npr.org/2022/06/21/1105848096/jan-6-committee-hearing-transcript.

[22] Frederick B. Jonassen, "Kiss the Book...You're President...: 'So Help Me God' and Kissing the Book in the Presidential Oath of Office," *William & Mary Bill of Rights Journal* 20, no. 3 (2012), https://scholarship.law.wm.edu/cgi/viewcontent.cgi?referer=&httpsredir=1&article=1614&context=wmborj.

[23] Steve Warren, "'We'll Be Praying for Him': Liz Cheney Responds to Democrat Critic Who Wants to Remove 'God,'" CBN, September 4, 2019, https://www2.cbn.com/news/politics/well-be-praying-him-liz-cheney-responds-democrat-critic-who-wants-remove-god.

[24] Warren, "'We'll Be Praying for Him.'"

people tell the truth by swearing to a deity they don't believe in. And we're definitely sure that such government oaths don't count as standing up for God—especially when some devout believers like many Mennonites specifically refuse to swear oaths because of Jesus's teachings in Matthew 5. But Cheney was speaking up for a form of Christian Nationalism, where the process of being allowed to serve as a congressional witness symbolically and rhetorically designates some people as not fully American citizens (and inherently untrustworthy) if they don't believe in God. Before Trump used Christian Nationalism to inspire people to storm the Capitol, Cheney was fighting to keep that potential ideology in power.

What's Next?

Rep. Liz Cheney serves as just one example of a mainline Protestant politician perpetuating Christian Nationalism. And Bishop Michael Curry represents just one example of a mainline Protestant leader who has preached against Christian Nationalism but still inadvertently helping advance the ideology. Countless others, emanating from both Republican and Democratic officials, could be highlighted. We could find sermons preached from mainline pulpits, even the most progressive ones, that do the same.

Our thesis about the twentieth-century history of mainline Protestantism being key to understanding the fervency of twenty-first century Christian Nationalism has been a topic of personal conversation for years. So we decided to send up a trial balloon. In January 2023, we published a piece in *Religion & Politics* titled "How Mainline Protestants Help Build Christian Nationalism."[25] We received positive feedback and affirmation from academics, mainline denominational leaders, and other pastors. Our editor seemed pleased with the number of eyeballs that landed on the piece. That led to conversations with Chalice Press about turning the argument into a book. In the chapters that follow, we will share stories that clearly reveal how the issue of Christian Nationalism does not reside solely within Trumpian circles or the churches that have vociferously

---

[25] Brian Kaylor and Beau Underwood, "How Mainline Protestants Help Build Christian Nationalism," *Religion & Politics*, January 4, 2023, https://religionandpolitics.org/2023/01/04/how-mainline-protestants-help-build-christian-nationalism.

embraced the former president. If we are honest, at times in our own ministries we have also been part of the problem.

In the rest of section one of this book, we will lay out the important theological foundation for our exploration. If you're not interested in the theological and philosophical issues about this topic, feel free to skim the next two chapters. The heart of the book is found in sections two and three. Chapter 2 outlines how Christian Nationalism is a heresy that distorts the gospel and leads Christians away from hearing and following the teachings of Jesus. This is why we capitalize the 'N' instead of using the more common style of "Christian nationalism." It warrants the same grammatical treatment as other religions, whose names we capitalize (like Buddhism, Hinduism, Islam). And it's why we spend time confronting this heretical co-option of our faith. Christian Nationalism isn't Christian. In chapter 3, we look back at the concept of civil religion, examining it from the illuminating hindsight of a post-January 6 insurrection world. We argue that what often was deemed harmless and enacted with good intentions instead helped pave the way to the hellish impacts of Christian Nationalism.

Section two of this book (chapters 4, 5, and 6) documents how mainline Protestants brought Christianity into government, baptizing the state in ways that prioritized their view of God, faith, and public life. Section three (chapters 7, 8, and 9) moves from the state to the church to show how mainline Protestants brought Christian Nationalism into churches, worship services, and denominational priorities. These two sections together show a comprehensive effort to merge church and state, thus setting the stage for Christian Nationalism that today inspires evangelicals and Pentecostals to storm the U.S. Capitol, push for Christian practices in public schools, and advocate for a host of other problematic mergers of God and country.

Finally, the last section of the book will continue to connect the dots between what mainline Protestants pushed for in the past and the problems facing our democracy and churches today. In this section, we will also lay out ways that mainline, evangelical, and other Christians can work to combat Christian Nationalism in their churches, communities, and nation. In an age of faith-fueled insurrections, this is the work to which God's people are called.

Chapter 2

A HERETICAL FAITH

Ahead of the 60th anniversary of the *Engel v. Vitale* decision by the U.S. Supreme Court that struck down government prayers in public schools, evangelist Franklin Graham argued Christians needed to take over school boards to make our nation better. And he argued that official prayer should've never been taken out of public schools.

"People have turned their backs on God," he declared on Fox News in 2022. "Our educators have taken God out of schools. Our politicians have taken God out of politics. Our nation is not better [for it]. Our nation is worse."[1]

Graham has picked up the mantle of his father, Billy Graham, who blasted the decision by the high court when it came out in 1962. That 6-1 ruling occurred after Jewish and secular families challenged the use of a prayer in their local New York school district. Each school day started with the same petition: "Almighty God, we acknowledge our dependence upon thee, and we beg thy blessings upon us, our parents, our teachers, and our country. Amen." The high court ruled that such a daily prayer constituted "a practice wholly inconsistent with the Establishment Clause."[2]

The Supreme Court's decision didn't end the controversy about prayer in public schools. In fact, it only intensified the conversation,

---

[1] Maureen Mackey, "Rev. Franklin Graham: School Board Member is 'Most Important Elected Official' in America Today," Fox News, April 19, 2022, https://www.foxnews.com/lifestyle/rev-franklin-graham-school-board-member-elected-official-america.

[2] *Engel v. Vitale*, 370 U.S. 421 (1962), https://supreme.justia.com/cases/federal/us/370/421/#tab-opinion-1943886.

one that continues more than six decades later as many politicians and preachers still insist the justices got it wrong. Prayer in public schools is such a resonating issue for those espousing Christian Nationalism today that sociologists Andrew Whitehead and Samuel Perry made it one of the six questions they ask when locating people on their Christian Nationalism scale, which ranges from those who reject the ideology to those who are ambassadors for it.[3]

"Ambassadors believe the United States has a special relationship with God, and thus, the federal government should formally declare the United States a Christian nation and advocate for Christian values," Whitehead and Perry explained. "Ambassadors support returning formal prayers to public schools and allowing the display of religious symbols in public spaces."[4]

But while Ambassadors like Graham long for the return of government prayer in public schools, few ask how the prayer got there in the first place. That story takes us not to 1962 but to 1951. The Board of Regents of New York tasked a group of clergy with penning a prayer that would be considered nondenominational but still imbue a desired moral instruction. They also connected it to nationalistic goals in a statement announcing the prayer: "We believe that at the commencement of each school day the act of allegiance to the flag might well be joined with this act of reverence to God."[5] Once the proposed language was made public, prominent mainline Protestant leaders quickly embraced it.

"Every patriotic and thoughtful citizen of all faiths should enthusiastically endorse the proposal," gushed Rev. Norman Vincent Peale of Manhattan's Marble Collegiate Church. "This country cannot endure if we cannot at least mention God in the schools."[6]

A Methodist minister leading a historic Reformed Church in America congregation, Peale would gain national fame the next year with his bestselling book *The Power of Positive Thinking*. A couple of years later he served as a vice president for the National Council of

---

[3] Andrew L. Whitehead and Samuel L. Perry, *Taking America back for God: Christian Nationalism in the United States*, (New York, NY: Oxford University Press, 2020).

[4] Whitehead and Perry, *Taking America Back for God*, 36.

[5] Mark Hanifin, "Prayer in Public Schools Backed By All But a Few," *The Tablet*, December 8, 1951, 21.

[6] Hanifin," Prayer in Public Schools."

Churches—and later became the longtime pastor of Donald Trump and officiated the future president's first wedding. Long before ambassadors of Christian Nationalism embraced Trump as he advocated for prayer in schools, Peale pushed the proposed classroom prayer in 1951 as "one of the most fundamental protections of American freedom that has been suggested in many a day."

Peale wasn't alone in his zeal. Mainline Protestant and Catholic ministers across the state were nearly unanimous in offering their support (and news reports occasionally noted opposition from Jewish clergy or secular leaders). Rev. Lauriston Scaife, the Episcopal bishop of Western New York, said, "I would certainly endorse it with enthusiasm. The overtones are highly significant for the times we live in."[7] Rev. Paul Heath, general presbyter for Presbyterians in Western New York, called the prayer "a splendid thing" and "acceptable to all faiths."[8] Rev. Dean Richardson, a Methodist pastor in Buffalo, praised it as "highly significant" and "in line with a trend that some of us have sensed all along—America is getting back to a new sense of sound spiritual values."[9] Even New York Gov. Thomas Dewey, an Episcopalian who had been the Democratic nominee for president in the previous two elections, backed the prayer: "In these days of worldwide conflict between the freed world and the slave world of godless communism, it is more vital than ever before that our children grow up with a sense of reverence and dedication to Almighty God."[10]

If it is now considered Christian Nationalism to advocate for official prayers in public schools, then it was also Christian Nationalism when Presbyterian, Episcopal, Lutheran, and Methodist clergy helped get such prayers into schools in the first place. This episode and others we will document throughout the book demonstrate that mainline Protestants need to reckon with their own history around Christian Nationalism. In ways both obvious and subtle, their beliefs and actions have advanced this ideology and created the fertile soil in which its most extreme versions now

---

[7] Hanifin, "Prayer in Public Schools."

[8] "Regents Proposal on School Prayer Wins Favor Here," *Buffalo News*, December 1, 1951, 3.

[9] "Proposal to Start School with Prayer Wins Support," *Buffalo Courier-Express*, December 1, 1951, 17.

[10] Hanifin, "Prayer in Public Schools."

bloom. As Taylor Swift sings in her song "Anti-Hero": "It's me, hi, I'm the problem, it's me."

The first step in that journey of introspection involves interrogating the theological problems of Christian Nationalism. We need to understand why this ideology poses such a threat. There may be a temptation to skip over this important work, but vaguely grasping that it's bad is insufficient. Those propagating these ideas are ready to marshal arguments in their defense. It's important to have theological explanations—and not just political critiques—for pushing back, whether those conversations are with Christian Nationalism's proponents or those mostly ignorant of its reality and effects.

American Idol

Anyone who spends even a cursory amount of time with the Bible will discover its condemnation of idolatry. The story of Israel, the teachings of Jesus, and the writings of early Christian communities serve as witnesses against this danger. It's right there in the Ten Commandments: "You shall not make for yourself an idol, whether in the form of anything that is in heaven above or that is on the earth beneath or that is in the water under the earth. You shall not bow down to them or serve them, for I the LORD your God am a jealous God" (Exodus 20:4–5a). And Paul spoke harshly about it to the Galatians:

> Formerly, when you did not know God, you were enslaved to beings that by nature are not gods. Now, however, that you have come to know God, or rather to be known by God, how can you turn back again to the weak and beggarly elemental principles? How can you want to be enslaved to them again? You are observing special days and months and seasons and years. I am afraid that my work for you may have been wasted. (Galatians 4:8–11)

Those are just two examples of many from Scripture that warn against the temptation to improperly put something else in God's place. Such a categorical mistake makes it impossible to live in a right relationship with God, each other, and the rest of creation. Idolatry distorts everything. These cautions are so numerous and severe because the impulse is constant and—like the Israelites in the desert who fashioned a golden calf out of their anxiety (Exodus 32:1–14)—many people who claim to worship God give into them. The danger is everywhere and it is hard to resist.

Paul Tillich, a Lutheran theologian and philosopher, defined faith "as the state of being ultimately concerned."[11] Whatever captures our ultimate concern, "demands the total surrender of [the person] who accepts this claim, and it promises total fulfillment even if all other claims have to be subjected to it or rejected in its name." In other words, the faith we hold is revealed by where we place our ultimate loyalty. When push comes to shove, what do we sacrifice all else for? Jesus makes it quite clear that in those moments God should be our ultimate concern (Matt. 6:24), but in practice Christians struggle with their fidelity. And the nation is often a seductive idol. With nationalism, Tillich explained, "everything is centered in the only god, the nation—a god who certainly proves to be a demon, but who shows clearly the unconditional character of an ultimate concern."[12] When the nation becomes the object of our faith, we imbue it with transcendent meaning and subsume our other loyalties, including our religious identities, to its demands.

Or, as H. Richard Niebuhr—another giant of twentieth-century mainline thought—argued, "Nationalism shows its character as a faith whenever national welfare or survival is regarded as the supreme end of life; whenever right and wrong are made dependent on the sovereign will of the nation, however determined; whenever religion and science, education and art, are valued by the measure of their contribution to national existence."[13]

This is exactly what Christian Nationalism expects of us. It transforms the nation into a sacred object that warrants unquestioned devotion. Critiques of the nation's historical actions or present decisions become grounds for excommunication. Instead of being patriots who want the United States to live up to its ideals, those questioning its actions are branded as "unAmerican." Rather than drawing on claims of transcendent truth to serve as a voice of con-

---

[11] Paul Tillich, *Dynamics of Faith* (New York: Perennial, 2001), 1–2.
[12] Tillich, *Dynamics of Faith*, 2.
[13] H. Richard Niebuhr, *Radical Monotheism and Western Culture* (Louisville: Westminster/John Knox, 1993), 27.

science, religion is instead used to baptize the nation and its leaders as divine servants, provided they're willing to follow the Christian Nationalist script. If they refuse to participate in the cultural myths or challenge the outdated social order, then they're portrayed as agents of evil or part of the demonic forces seeking to destroy America.

Tillich and Niebuhr have proven prophetic, but they are far from the only people whose ideas challenge Christian Nationalism on theological grounds. Contemporary Christian voices echo their warnings against misplacing one's faith in a nation constructed and led by fallible humans. Conservative political scientist Paul Miller cautioned:

> The ideal type of Christian Nationalism cannot go together with Christianity: they are separate, rival, mutually exclusive religions. They make fundamentally incommensurable claims on human loyalty. ... Nationalism is a totalistic political religion that is inconsistent with orthodox Christianity, a false religion that places the nation in the place of the church and the leader in place of God.[14]

Similarly, Russell Moore, the former head of the Southern Baptist Convention's public policy arm who now leads the leading evangelical magazine *Christianity Today*, argued, "Christian Nationalism is not a politically enthusiastic version of Christianity, nor is it a religiously informed patriotism. Christian Nationalism is a prosperity gospel for nation-states, a liberation theology for White people."[15]

The consequences of this mistake are profound for the witness of Christ's Church and those who belong to it. As Catholic theologian William Cavanaugh suggested in his critique of combining a belief in American exceptionalism and God's providential activity throughout history:

> The church as mediator between God and America—a church that has the critical distance to pronounce judgment as well as blessing—is in danger of being erased. What has happened in effect is that America has become the new church. When the relationship of America and God is thus

---

[14] Paul Miller, *The Religion of American Greatness: What's Wrong with Christian Nationalism* (Downers Grove: IVP Academic, 2022), 142.

[15] Russell Moore, *Losing Our Religion: An Altar Call for Evangelical America* (New York: Sentinel, 2023), 117.

direct, there is little to check the identification of God's will with America's. America is God's people, the bearer of God's salvation to the world.[16]

With the church not acting as an "irritant" in the "body politic," he added, we see people "transfer the sovereignty of God to the sovereign state."

In idolizing the nation, Christian Nationalism makes two grave errors. First, it portrays flawed human governments and their leaders as divine agents, rendering them godlike and worthy of a devotion that properly belongs only to God. Second, it reduces the church to a servant of the nation, sapping it of the authority to help discern what does (and does not) serve the common good. It deprives religious communities of their ability to act as a moral conscience within society, while instead justifying unconscionable activities undertaken by a state as sacred causes.

Not in God's Image

A basic Christian affirmation is that human life is sacred. We enjoy a special status in God's creation, as we were made a little lower than the angels so that we might be co-laborers with God (Psalm 8:5-6). In describing this elevated place, Genesis beautifully states that each of us is created in the image of God (1:27). Jesus teaches that our care for the most vulnerable reflects how we treat him because in them we encounter Christ (Matthew 25:31-46).

We reference these foundational claims so often that they risk becoming rote. We should not lose perspective on how radical these ideas truly were both in biblical times and for us now. At a moment in human history when power was highly concentrated among ruling elites, the claim that humans bore the image of a divine ruler had revolutionary implications. Here's how biblical scholar J. Richard Middleton unpacked this:

> All human beings, male and female, are created as God's royal stewards in the world, entrusted with the privileged task

---

[16] William Cavanaugh, *Migrations of the Holy: God, State, and the Political Meaning of the Church* (Grand Rapids: Eerdmans, 2011), 104-105.

of ruling on God's behalf (1:26–28). The democratization of the *imago Dei* in Genesis 1 thus constitutes an implicit delegitimation of the entire ruling and priestly structure of Mesopotamian society (and especially the absolute power of the king). In the Genesis version, it is ordinary humans (and not some elite class) who are understood to be significant historical actors in the arena of earthly life.[17]

The announcement that humans bear God's image and serve as God's representatives was a statement about human equality. Instead of some—the political and religious elites—counting as more than others, Genesis emphasizes that all have the same worth and dignity due to their common Creator. That truth about our shared source of life overwhelms and overrides any differences in earthly status. *From* the beginning, the Bible tells us that what happened *in* the beginning determines how we should regard and relate to each other as human beings. This ancient truth resonates deeply given the divisions and disparities that define our contemporary world.

Faithfulness to God today still involves, as Christian writer Lisa Sharon Harper described it, "the honoring of the image of God in all humanity—every single human on earth. It is the renouncing of the lies the world tells us that some people are created with more of the image of God than others—more call and capacity to exercise dominion than others—more call and capacity to steward the world—that is the core spiritual lie of our age. The gospel comes against that lie."[18] Christian Nationalism buys into this "core spiritual lie." It denies the equality of each person and degrades the image of God in those it regards as less than others.

Over and over, social scientists have found a troubling association between strong expressions of Christian Nationalism and a variety of retrograde viewpoints. The attempt to defend a social order that privileges power for straight White men and a moral traditionalism that regards this hierarchy as divinely ordained conflicts with what Scripture teaches about the status of humans before God and in relation to each other. For example, White Americans who report

---

[17] J. Richard Middleton, *The Liberating Image: The* Imago Dei *in Genesis 1* (Grand Rapids: Brazos, 2005), 204.

[18] Brian McLaren, "An Interview with Lisa Sharon Harper," June 16, 2016, https://brianmclaren.net/an-interview-with-lisa-sharon-harper.

stronger Christian Nationalist beliefs are less likely to acknowledge racial injustices in society toward minority groups; instead, they report higher beliefs of discrimination against White people.[19] They are also more politically tolerant of racism relative to White people who express less agreement with Christian Nationalistic ideas.[20] Similarly, researchers found a statistically significant association between greater support for Christian Nationalism and increased opposition to interracial marriage.[21]

The racism in Christian Nationalism today is important to recognize. That's why many scholars, ministers, and activists rightly talk about the ideology as White Christian Nationalism. Anthea Butler, author of *White Evangelical Racism*, therefore defined the ideology in a report on Christian Nationalism's role in the Capitol insurrection as "the belief that America's founding is based on Christian principles, White Protestant Christianity is the operational religion of the land, and that Christianity should be the foundation of how the nation develops its laws, principles, and policies."[22] If the U.S. was founded as a "Christian" nation, as those pushing this ideology insist, then it was at best a nation only for White Christians, given the genocide of Native American peoples and the enslavement of African American peoples by the founders. Returning to such roots doesn't seem "Christian" to us, but it is definitely a Eurocentric ideal. That answers the question Butler posed along with her definition: "What kind of Christianity, and what kind of nationalism?" As Jemar Tisby, author of *The Color of Compromise*, added in the same report on Christian Nationalism and January 6, "The White Christian Nationalist version of patriotism

[19] Samuel Perry, Ryan Cobb, Andrew Whitehead, and Joshua Grubbs, "Divided by Faith (in Christian America): Christian Nationalism, Race, and Divergent Perceptions of Racial Injustice," *Social Forces* 101, no. 2 (December 2022): 913, https://doi.org/10.1093/sf/soab134.

[20] Joshua Davis and Samuel Perry, "White Christian Nationalism and Relative Political Tolerance for Racists," *Social Problems* 68, no. 3 (August 2021): 513, https://doi.org/10.1093/socpro/spaa002.

[21] Samuel Perry and Andrew Whitehead, "Christian Nationalism and White Racial Boundaries: Examining Whites' Opposition to Interracial Marriage," *Ethnic and Racial Studies* 38, no. 10 (March 2015): 1671, https://doi.org/10.1080/01419870.2015.1015584.

[22] Anthea Butler, "What is White Christian Nationalism?" in *Christian Nationalism and the January 6, 2021 Insurrection*, 4, https://bjconline.org/wp-content/uploads/2022/02/Christian_Nationalism_and_the_Jan6_Insurrection-2-9-22.pdf.

is racist, xenophobic, patriarchal, and exclusionary. Their vision of the nation conveniently puts White people—especially men—who are politically conservative and who make some claim of Christian adherence at the top of the social hierarchy."[23] For Christians who seek to be anti-racist—as some mainline Protestants profess as a goal—the danger of Christian Nationalistic ideas runs deeper than just issues of church and state. It can also undermine work in areas to confront racism, misogyny, and other heresies.

Or consider the relationship between Christian Nationalism and support for basic rights. The insurrection on January 6, 2021, was an extreme example of the anti-democratic goals of Christian Nationalism. But it doesn't stop there. It also fuels efforts today to prevent some people from voting. Those expressing agreement with Christian Nationalistic ideas are more willing to limit access to the ballot box.[24] They are also less concerned with protecting free speech and freedom of the press. The ability to learn what is happening, speak out, and vote on an equal basis is a pillar of democratic life.[25] Restricting this for some makes the obvious statement that all people are not valued in the same way.

Religion scholar Bradley Onishi argued in *Preparing for War: The Extremist History of White Christian Nationalism—And What Comes Next*:

> In many ways, it's no surprise that the group who believed—
> and still believes—it has an inherent right to power over the
> nation sees democracy as unfortunate collateral damage in
> their culture war. If the will of the people needs to be left
> behind in order to remake America as the city on a hill, then

[23] Jemar Tisby, "The Patriotic Witness of Black Christians," in *Christian Nationalism and the January 6, 2021 Insurrection*, 7, https://bjconline.org/wp-content/uploads/2022/02/Christian_Nationalism_and_the_Jan6_Insurrection-2-9-22.pdf.

[24] Samuel Perry, Andrew Whitehead, and Joshua Grubbs, "I Don't Want Everybody to Vote": Christian Nationalism and Restricting Voter Access in the United States," *Sociological Forum* 37, no. 1 (March 2022): 4, https://doi.org/10.1111/socf.12776.

[25] Joshua Davis, Samuel Perry, and Joshua Grubbs, "Liberty for Us, Limits for Them: Christian Nationalism and Americans' Views on Citizens' Rights," *Sociology of Religion*, (May 2023): srac044, https://doi.org/10.1093/socrel/srac044.

so be it. The goal is to retake the country for God, even if the republic has to be martyred in the process.[26]

That is why Rev. Paul Raushenbush, an American Baptist minister who leads the Interfaith Alliance, insists that "Christian Nationalism is a threat to the American way of life."[27] As he explained, "It's important to recognize [religious diversity is] fundamentally a strength for America, not a threat. This circle has to include everyone. White Christians don't get to say, 'This is our country and the rest are lucky to be invited.'"

A final data point involves the role of violence in maintaining social order. Based on original survey research conducted in the month after the attack on the U.S. Capitol, a group of political scientists found how Christian Nationalism—in connection with White identity, perceived victimhood, and a belief in conspiracy theories—is associated with greater support for political violence.[28] In this framework, violence becomes a necessary tool, especially racist violence against Black Americans. Coercion may be a necessary means to achieve ends that are perceived as worthy but fail to recognize everyone as equal in the eyes of God. Sociologists Philip Gorski and Samuel Perry explained the worldview this way: "Order is understood in a hierarchical way, with White Christian men at the top. And violence is seen as a righteous means of defending freedom and restoring order, means that are reserved to White Christian men."[29]

In total, these findings provide persuasive evidence that Christian Nationalism undermines the ability to see and respect

---

[26] Bradley Onishi, *Preparing for War: The Extremist History of White Christian Nationalism—And What Comes Next* (Minneapolis: Broadleaf Books, 2023), 136.

[27] Yonat Shimron, "Paul Raushenbush: 'Christian Nationalism Is a Threat to the American Way of Life,'" *Religion News Service*, July 22, 2022, https://religionnews.com/2022/07/22/paul-raushenbush-christian-nationalism-is-a-threat-to-the-american-way-of-life.

[28] Miles Armaly, David Buckley, and Adam Enders, "Christian Nationalism and Political Violence: Victimhood, Racial Identity, Conspiracy, and Support for the Capitol Attacks," *Political Behavior* 44 (January 2022): 937, https://doi.org/10.1007/s11109-021-09758-y.

[29] Philip Gorski and Samuel Perry, *The Flag and the Cross: White Christian Nationalism and the Threat to American Democracy* (New York: Oxford, 2022), 7.

the image of God in other people. Instead of seeing each life as sacred, the beliefs within this cultural framework about how society should be structured create the justification to view and treat people unequally.

The Opposite of Good News

In addition to making the nation into an idol and denying the image of God in human beings, Christian Nationalism suffers from another fatal flaw: it contradicts the basic teachings of Jesus. There's no good news in the gospel it preaches. In the biblical story, Jesus isn't just crucified by the Roman Empire and raised by the power of God. He spends years preaching and teaching a compelling way of life. He calls his followers to conform themselves to this way. He gathers a community around him committed to manifesting the reign of God that he announces.

"The 'kingdom of God' is a way of talking about the restoration of creation through God's will being done in this world in the same way that God's will is accomplished in heaven," wrote theologian Frederick Christian Bauerschmidt. "What Jesus calls the good news is his proclamation that this is beginning to come to pass, the kingdom is drawing near. It is drawing near in the words and actions of Jesus himself."[30]

Convinced that Christian Nationalism is antithetical to this message, Andrew Whitehead—one of the leading social scientists studying Christian Nationalism in the United States—passionately testified about the incongruities between this ideology and what Jesus reveals about the ways of God. In his book *American Idolatry: How Christian Nationalism Betrays the Gospel and Threatens the Church*, he identified three major points of dissonance.

The first is how Christian Nationalism uses power, which involves achieving one's goals despite opposition from others. It seeks power because, in Whitehead's words, its final goal "rests in safeguarding a space where White, culturally and religiously conservative, natural-born citizens occupy the unquestioned center of the culture and enjoy privileged access to interpersonal,

---

[30] Frederick Christian Bauerschmidt, *The Love That is God: An Invitation to Christian Faith* (Grand Rapids: Eerdmans, 2020), 30.

organizational, and institutional control."[31] Power is the means to the end of imposing a particular social order. In a country where demographics are rapidly changing, associations between Christian Nationalist beliefs and support for voting restrictions demonstrate the desire to limit who has the power to influence the direction of the country. Rather than using power to serve others and protect the dignity of all, Christian Nationalism sees it as a tool to force others to abide by its restrictive desires for society.

The second divergence is fear. By making people feel like they are constantly under threat from the racial, immigrant, or non-Christian "other," Christian Nationalism provokes people to act in ways that are decidedly unlike Jesus. Instead of trusting Scripture's words to "fear not," this cultural framework seeks danger lurking in any deviation from a world where straight, cisgender White men run the show. Instead of stirring hope and compassion, it feeds despair and incites us to cruelty.

Finally, Whitehead calls out the embrace of violence. While Jesus is the Prince of Peace, Christian Nationalism makes it much easier to condone violence. There's a certain logic to it: if you believe society is disintegrating, then violence becomes necessary to restore order. Of course, the history of Christian rationalization of violence is an ugly one. It reveals humans are much more convicted about obtaining and preserving power than about actually being peacemakers.

Collectively, these tendencies indicate a much larger problem. Committing their lives to following Jesus and serving God's ways should lead Christians into a distinctive set of practices that challenge the dominant ethos of our culture. Christian Nationalism leads would-be followers of Jesus in the opposite direction, while grossly misrepresenting Christianity to everyone else. It preaches a false message that undermines the work of discipleship and the Church's witness to the world. As Whitehead aptly put it, "[Christian Nationalism] creates disciples who are more concerned with ensuring they control the center of the culture than standing with those on the margins. Instead of advocating being counted among

---

[31] Andrew Whitehead, *American Idolatry: How Christian Nationalism Betrays the Gospel and Threatens the Church,* (Grand Rapids: Brazos, 2023), 52.

the lowly, White Christian Nationalism requires stepping on the lowly in order to be counted."[32]

Voices in the Wilderness

Even as expressions of Christian Nationalism in our politics and our churches may be intensifying, they are not going unchallenged. Aware of the damage they pose to both American democracy and the gospel Jesus preached, important voices within American Christianity are pushing back. One of the most prominent efforts has been the launching of "Christians Against Christian Nationalism." Organized by the Baptist Joint Committee for Religious Liberty, the campaign seeks to offer a witness countering those seeking to merge American and Christian identities. The group released a statement in 2019 endorsed by prominent Christian leaders, including many who guide mainline Protestant denominations and institutions. The statement explains:

> As Christians, our faith teaches us everyone is created in God's image and commands us to love one another. As Americans, we value our system of government and the good that can be accomplished in our constitutional democracy. Today, we are concerned about a persistent threat to both our religious communities and our democracy—Christian Nationalism. ... It often overlaps with and provides cover for White supremacy and racial subjugation. We reject this damaging political ideology and invite our Christian brothers and sisters to join us in opposing this threat to our faith and to our nation.[33]

That prophetic critique against Christian Nationalism came a year and a half before the January 6, 2021, insurrection and helped prepare the way to expose this heretical ideology. BJC Executive Director Amanda Tyler has been a prominent voice explaining and condemning Christian Nationalism, speaking in local churches across the country and regularly appearing in media stories and TV segments on the topic.

---

[32] Whitehead, *American Idolatry*, 180.
[33] "Christians Against Christian Nationalism," Christians Against Christian Nationalism, https://www.christiansagainstchristiannationalism.org/statement.

Others have joined BJC in sounding the alarm. The 2023 General Assembly of the Christian Church (Disciples of Christ) passed a resolution denouncing Christian Nationalism as antithetical "to the very heart of the Christian Church (Disciples of Christ) identity by promoting division and stratification of the human family to the detriment of the unity and equality that our baptisms beget (Galatians 3:28) and the Lord's Table celebrates (1 Corinthians 11:17-34)." It resolved, "The Church calls on its leaders and members to take every possible opportunity to speak out and act boldly against Christian Nationalism, ensuring that the love of God known to us in Jesus Christ may not be distorted by this ugly and false appropriation of our faith, but proclaimed with generosity and grace to all peoples, from our doorsteps to the ends of the earth."[34]

Beyond these official channels, other mainline leaders are vocal in their opposition to Christian Nationalism. They mobilize and speak as people within a tradition, even if they are not authorized representatives of it. One example is Rev. Jennifer Butler, a Presbyterian Church (U.S.A.) pastor and the founder of Faith in Public Life. In recent years, Butler has traveled across the country speaking at major events and in local church sanctuaries about Christian Nationalism and how to counter its effects.

"We need to speak boldly from our specific faith traditions to counter the rhetoric of religious nationalists even as we model a respect for all faiths. We cannot cede the language of faith to autocrats who perpetuate this outrageous lie that human rights and democracy are antithetical to faith rather than the fulfillment of our religious values," she argued in 2023 during the Parliament of the World's Religions.[35]

In contrast to Christian Nationalism's ideology, Butler's ministry focuses on "helping faith leaders understand that their religious freedom entitles them to speak from a Jewish voice, a Catholic voice,

---

[34] "GA-2341," General Assembly 2023, Christian Church (Disciples of Christ), https://ga.disciples.org/resolutions/2023/ga-2341.

[35] Jennifer Butler, "The Global Christian Nationalist Threat to Democracy and Freedom," *Reclaiming Faith*, August 18, 2023, https://revjenbutler.substack.com/p/the-global-christian-nationalist.

a Muslim voice, and that that voice actually helps people understand what's happening in the world today."[36]

Another important voice in this space is Rev. Nathan Empsall, an Episcopal priest who leads Faithful America. Through that organization, he has led petition drives in protest of leaders espousing Christian Nationalistic ideas and coordinated counterprogramming to events like the ReAwaken America Tour (or RAT for short; see chapter 11 for details of its spiritual bankruptcy).

"The goal of Christian Nationalism is clear: to seize political power for its conservative Christian adherents at all costs and at the expense of all others," he said at a press conference in Florida in advance of a RAT stop happening at Trump National Doral in Miami, Florida. "That's not a religion—it is a political ideology. One that co-opts the symbols and rhetoric of religion, but only co-opts them and does not start with them."[37]

Grassroots efforts to learn about and stand against Christian Nationalism are also popping up. Churches are hosting experts and activists for forums and education sessions. Pastors—either on their own or in organized efforts[38]—are preaching sermons to alert their flocks. Mainline Protestants and other Christians are rising to meet this challenge. These theological critiques are signs of hope. Christians are reminding themselves of their core beliefs and pushing back against the forces warping their faith. For some, speaking out has proven costly in terms of maintaining positions of influence or keeping people in the pews. The willingness to take such risks to confront this evil is inspiring. It should not go unheralded.

At the same time, denunciations of others in the present moment by mainline Protestants are insufficient. Fully addressing the problem will require interrogating their own respective histories to

---

[36] Erik Gunn, "Warning Wisconsin People of Faith about White Christian Nationalism," *Wisconsin Examiner*, February 7, 2023, https://wisconsinexaminer.com/2023/02/07/warning-wisconsin-people-of-faith-about-white-christian-nationalism.

[37] Jeremy Fuzy, "Christian Leaders Continue Opposition to ReAwaken America Tour—at Trump Resort," *Word&Way*, May 12, 2023, https://wordandway.org/2023/05/12/christian-leaders-continue-opposition-to-reawaken-america-tour.

[38] Brian Kaylor and Beau Underwood, "Preachers United Against Christian Nationalism," *A Public Witness*, October 13, 2022, https://publicwitness.wordandway.org/p/preachers-united-against-christian.

understand how their past words and actions contributed to what's unfolding now. Heartfelt repentance is needed alongside prophetic condemnations. This book seeks to create that conversation and make those critical discussions possible. Before we dive into the specific history of mainline Protestantism and Christian Nationalism, there's another pernicious influence we need to name and understand. While mainline Protestants aided the rise of Christian Nationalism, the tradition of American civil religion opened the gate to do so.

Chapter 3

(UN)CIVIL RELIGION

On March 15, 1965, President Lyndon Johnson stood in the U.S. House Chamber to deliver a special message to a joint session of Congress. He spoke four days after Rev. James Reeb, a Presbyterian-turned-Unitarian Universalist minister, had been killed in Selma, Alabama, where he had traveled to join marches in support of civil rights. Reeb's death, which garnered more national attention than the murders of Black civil rights activists also killed, gave urgency to Johnson's push for a voting rights bill. So Johnson stood before lawmakers to note the violence in Selma and how "one good man, a man of God, was killed."[1]

As Johnson made his case for voting rights for Black people, he quickly turned to the Bible:

> Rarely are we met with a challenge, not to our growth or abundance, our welfare or our security, but rather to the values and the purposes and the meaning of our beloved nation. The issue of equal rights for American Negroes is such an issue. And should we defeat every enemy, should we double our wealth and conquer the stars, and still be unequal to this issue, then we will have failed as a people and as a nation. For with a country as with a person, "What is a man profited, if he shall gain the whole world, and lose his own soul?"

---

[1] Lyndon B. Johnson, "Special Message to the Congress: The American Promise," March 15, 1965, https://www.presidency.ucsb.edu/documents/special-message-the-congress-the-american-promise.

After invoking the nation's soul and quoting Jesus to back the legislation, Johnson also made the argument even more explicitly that God supported the voting rights legislation: "The time of justice has now come. I tell you that I believe sincerely that no force can hold it back. It is right in the eyes of man and God that it should come." Johnson returned to that argument to close his appeal for the legislation, while also ordaining the lawmakers as God's holy agents seeking to do God's will.

"Above the pyramid on the great seal of the United States it says—in Latin—'God has favored our undertaking,'" Johnson declared. "God will not favor everything that we do. It is rather our duty to divine his will. But I cannot help believing that he truly understands and that he really favors the undertaking that we begin here tonight."

This speech by Johnson appears in a significant essay by sociologist Robert Bellah as an exemplar of "civil religion." For Bellah, civil religion is "a collection of beliefs, symbols, and rituals with respect to sacred things and institutionalized in a collectivity."[2] He believed that such a collection is important since "any coherent and viable society rests on a common set of moral understandings about good and bad, right and wrong, in the realm of individual and social action."[3] He insisted that "these common moral understandings must also in turn rest upon a common set of religious understandings that provide a picture of the universe in terms of which the moral understandings make sense."

All of this, for Bellah, meant "civil religion is indispensable" and "absolutely integral" to "our existence as a republican people."[4] And he set such civil religion in contrast to religious nationalism. So he pointed to Johnson's God-talk in the voting rights speech as a "recent illustration" to prove "American civil religion is still very much alive."[5] But we wouldn't call it "civil religion" if Donald Trump had stood before a joint session, urged support for his ban on people from Muslim nations entering the country, and declared that God

[2] Robert N. Bellah, *The Broken Covenant: America Civil Religion in Time of Trial* (Chicago: University of Chicago Press, 1992), 104.

[3] Robert N. Bellah, *The Broken Covenant: America Civil Religion in Time of Trial* (New York: Seabury Press, 1975), ix.

[4] Bellah, *The Broken Covenant*, 1992, 176, 179.

[5] Robert N. Bellah, "Civil Religion in America." *Daedalus* 96, no. 1 (1967): 13.

favored the bill so therefore lawmakers should fulfill their moral duty by supporting the legislation. Yet, the definition of Christian Nationalism can't just be God-talk with which we politically disagree. So having defined Christian Nationalism and how it is problematic in the previous two chapters, we need to take a moment to also address the concept of "civil religion," since some people use that label to describe the work of mainline Protestants in creating Christian Nationalism.

The Doctrine of Civil Religion

For most of his seminal essay defining civil religion, Bellah looked to history. He rightly noted that the U.S. founders did not try to create the U.S. as a "Christian" nation and instead used religion in ways he referred to as "civil religion." Like generations of scholars between him and us, we find his historical analysis convincing. He clearly captured something important about how the founders talked about a "Creator," "Providence," and "Nature's God." This concept of civil religion reflects "a genuine apprehension of universal and transcendent religious reality as seen in or, one could almost say, as revealed through the experience of the American people."[6] Yet, such participation in the sacred through one's citizenship does not involve "the worship of the American nation but an understanding of the American experience in the light of ultimate and universal reality."[7]

At the same time, civil religion does not replace personal faith commitments. Instead, it expresses shared national values that are distinct from sectarian beliefs. Bellah argued there are "certain common elements of religious orientation that the great majority of Americans share. These have played a crucial role in the development of American institutions and still provide a religious dimension for the whole fabric of American life, including the political sphere."[8] While noting this difference, Bellah suggested that civil religion "borrowed selectively from [Christianity in the early United States] in such a way that the average American saw no conflict between the two. In this way, the civil religion was able to build up without any bitter struggle with the church powerful symbols of national solidarity and to mobilize deep levels of personal motivation for the

---

[6] Bellah, "Civil Religion," 1967, 12.
[7] Bellah, "Civil Religion," 1967, 18.
[8] Bellah, "Civil Religion," 1967, 3–4.

attainment of national goals."[9] Thus, he identified several Christian themes that became nationalist tools as part of civic occasions and ceremonies. America was portrayed as a new promised land. Both individual citizens and the collective nation were called to perform God's will. There were references to redemptive suffering, secular martyrs, and a God who is "actively interested and involved in history, with a special concern for America."[10]

Through rituals and rhetoric, the nation's past trials and present pursuits could be imbued with sacred significance. A diverse people could be united in common purpose and motivated by a sense that they were accountable to something larger than themselves. The state may be organized and run by humans, but an unspecified deity would evaluate its actions. All of this may seem rather abstract, but illumination can be found by looking at one particular way civil religion operates.

In his book *American Covenant*, sociologist Philip Gorski traced the presence of civil religion within U.S. history. Starting with the Puritans, he identified covenant as a major concept of this tradition:

> The Puritans debated [covenant's] meaning, but they agreed on its significance: it was the central node that held together a cluster of interrelated ideas—chosenness, godliness, and civility, to name a few. The result was a web of meaning strong enough to hold the Bay Colony together during its formative years and elastic enough to encompass the nation as a whole during later years.[11]

In his articulation and defense of civil religion, Gorski sought to differentiate the concept as a middle ground between two problematic understandings of how religion and politics should relate. If civil religion imbues a nation with transcendent meaning that unites all people in common cause, danger lurks in "radical secularism" that restricts religious expression and ideas solely to the private sphere and in "religious nationalism" that finds animation in conquest and fear.[12] While Gorski believes there's a value civil religion

---

[9] Bellah, "Civil Religion," 1967, 13.
[10] Bellah, "Civil Religion," 1967, 7.
[11] Philip Gorski, *American Covenant: A History of Civil Religion from the Puritans to the Present* (Princeton: Princeton University Press, 2017), 59.
[12] Gorski, *American Covenant*, 18.

offers to public life, he's also clearly aware of the risks religious (or, specifically, Christian) nationalism poses. For all the instrumental value religious ideals, imagery, and language can offer in instilling people with a shared purpose and providing a populace with a common meaning, there's a long history of combining religion with the state to stoke division and justify violence.

Bellah himself warned of this risk: "The civil religion has not always been invoked in favor of worthy causes. On the domestic scene, an American-Legion type of ideology that fuses God, country, and flag has been used to attack nonconformist and liberal ideas and groups of all kinds." Speaking to the downside of seeing the United States as God's chosen nation, he also named how this self-understanding serves the cause of conquest: "The theme of the American Israel was used, almost from the beginning, as a justification for the shameful treatment of the Indians so characteristic of our history. It can be overtly or implicitly linked to the idea of manifest destiny which has been used to legitimate several adventures in imperialism since the early nineteenth century."[13]

Things Fall Apart

While Bellah, Gorski, and many other scholars show the unifying nature of American civil religion (even with its dark side that unified a White Christian majority), the increasing religious pluralism of American society challenges a foundational premise of civil religion, which could render it an unrealistic dream from yesteryear. As Bellah explained, "The civil religion has been a point of articulation between the profoundest commitments of the Western religious and philosophical tradition and the common beliefs of ordinary Americans."[14] What happens when "ordinary Americans" no longer share "common beliefs" or understand the "commitments of the Western religious and philosophical tradition"? The traditional understanding of civil religion operates on the assumption of a shared religious and philosophical framework. For the ideas of "covenant" or the U.S. as a "new Israel" to inspire and unify the country, the reference must be understood and considered meaningful by the public. As the cultural influence of Christianity wanes and such biblical allusions are less salient in people's minds, it

---

[13] Bellah, "Civil Religion," 1967, 14.
[14] Bellah, "Civil Religion," 1967, 15–16.

becomes harder for civil religion to play the positive role that Bellah and Gorski assign to it. Perhaps it supported the common good in the past, but current sociological trends portend a very different future.

Consider the shift in religious demographics since the publication of Bellah's piece on civil religion in 1967. According to Gallup, 92% of Americans identified as Christian in 1967.[15] That left 3% as Jewish, 3% as another faith, and only 2% claiming no faith. In terms of demographics, the U.S. was basically a nation of Christians. And it was particularly a nation of Protestants with more than two-thirds of Americans claiming that label. By 2022, the picture changed significantly. A majority still identified as Christian (68%), but that meant one-third of the population did not claim that label. While the Jewish population held mostly steady (2%), the number claiming another faith grew (8%) and those claiming no religion skyrocketed (21%). If those trends continue, the U.S. could in a couple of decades become a nation where fewer than half of the population claims Christianity. With such religious diversity, a covenant or civil religion borrowing from Christian symbols and language not only will resonate with fewer people but will also no longer serve as unifying for the nation. If a civil religious alternative to religious nationalism can flourish in a healthy way for a nation, that era is in the past for the United States. Bellah's covenant has expired. Attempts at civil religion today might not function much differently in practicality from Christian Nationalism as both define a growing swatch of U.S. citizens as not fundamentally part of what Bellah saw as "the American Way of Life."

This demographic shift shouldn't be underestimated. Not only does it undermine the ability of civil religion to function as a unifying force, but it also animates Christian Nationalism among conservative evangelicals today. As historian Kristin Kobes Du Mez, author of *Jesus and John Wayne*, explained in 2023 as she discussed the anti-democratic attitudes among those espousing Christian Nationalism: "I think what has escalated things in the last decade or so is a growing alarm among conservative White Christians that they no longer have numbers on their side. So looking at the demographic change in this country, the quote-unquote 'end of White Christian

---

[15] "Religion," Gallup, https://news.gallup.com/poll/1690/religion.aspx.

America,' and there's where you can see a growing willingness to blatantly abandon any commitment to democracy."[16] Worried that demographics are destiny, some politicians and preachers today seek not a unifying civil religion but a polarizing and discriminatory Christian Nationalism.

As we'll show in the upcoming chapters, civil religion was giving way to Christian Nationalism before Bellah published his important essay. So while we think he described something significant, we quibble with his interpretation of what were then current events as he insisted this civil religious construct remained in place. He started his 1967 piece by looking at the few "God" references in John F. Kennedy's inaugural address. But perhaps the rhetoric of the nation's first Catholic president didn't actually echo the mostly Protestant nation's public discourse on religion. After all, different religious traditions talk about their faith differently, which impacts how presidents talk about religion.[17]

Bellah could have looked to a different president to reach a different conclusion. As we'll see in the next chapter, Dwight D. Eisenhower offered quite a different approach in his 1953 inaugural address that we argue wasn't civil religion but Christian Nationalism. But Bellah's sole line from Eisenhower is a misquoted statement used to suggest the former general had a vague religiosity. Bellah's source for the Eisenhower quote got it wrong and thus misinterpreted what Ike said, an error Bellah repeated. After highlighting Kennedy's vague God references, Bellah wrote, "Isn't Eisenhower reported to have said, 'Our government makes no sense unless it is founded in a deeply felt religious faith—and I don't care what it is,' and isn't that a complete negation of any real religion?"[18] It is true Eisenhower was reported as having said that. But as scholar Patrick Henry later documented, the report Bellah relied on is a misquote and included an out-of-context misinterpretation of Eisenhower's poorly-

[16] Katelyn Fossett, "'He Seems to be Saying His Commitment Is to Minority Rule,'" *Politico*, October 27, 2023, https://www.politico.com/news/magazine/2023/10/27/mike-johnson-christian-nationalist-ideas-qa-00123882.

[17] Brian T. Kaylor, *Presidential Campaign Rhetoric in an Age of Confessional Politics* (Lanham: Lexington Books, 2011).

[18] Bellah, "Civil Religion," 1967, 3.

phrased, unscripted comment.[19] Speaking a few weeks before his inauguration, the president-elect tried to explain why he found it difficult to explain democracy to someone from the Soviet Union:

> I was quite certain it was hopeless on my part to talk to him about the fact that our form of government is founded in religion. Our ancestors who formed this government said in order to explain it, you remember, that a decent respect for the opinion of mankind impels them to declare the reasons which led to the separation [from Britain]. And this is how they explained those: We hold 'that all men are endowed by their Creator,' not by the accident of birth, not by the color of their skins or by anything else, but 'all men are endowed by their Creator.' In other words, our form of government has no sense unless it is founded in a deeply felt religious faith, and I don't care what it is. With us, of course, it is the Judeo-Christian concept, but it must be a religion that all men are created equal. So what was the use of me talking to [a Soviet acquaintance] about that? Religion, he had been taught, was the opiate of the people.[20]

Eisenhower wasn't really talking about religion—and certainly wasn't trying to negate real religion. He was trying to explain democracy. And for him, democracy needed a religious foundation to explain why all people were created equal, a key concept he believed was needed to ensure a democracy where all people have equal rights. His famous "I don't care what it is" line wasn't about his religion or even the dominant religion in the U.S. but about democracy more broadly and philosophically. He seemed to acknowledge that a democracy elsewhere could be based on a different religion, like perhaps a Jewish or Buddhist democracy. But then he quickly added that he believed U.S. democracy was founded on what he called "Judeo-Christian" faith and thus only with such religion did U.S. democracy work. As we'll show in the next chapter, Eisenhower would embody a more sectarian vision of democracy the next month during his inauguration. Far from trying to negate

---

[19] Patrick Henry, "'And I Don't Care What It Is,': The Tradition-History of a Civil Religion Proof-Text," *Journal of the American Academy of Religion* 49, no. 1 (1981): 35–49.

[20] Henry, "'And I Don't Care What It Is,'" 41.

religion, Eisenhower would soon lead a Christian revival within U.S. public life that looked less like civil religion and far more like Christian Nationalism.

Additionally, we take issue with some of the other examples Bellah pointed to as "civil religion," including "the motto, 'In God we trust,' as well as the inclusion of the phrase 'under God' in the Pledge to the flag."[21] As we'll argue in the next section, we find these instead to represent Christian Nationalistic features that continue to impact our political and religious life today.

So while we think Bellah captured something important, we also believe many things called "civil religion" (and thus treated as harmless) in the years since his essay actually reflect and operate as Christian Nationalism. And as we'll show in the upcoming chapters, these Christian Nationalistic efforts were often put into place by mainline Protestants who thought their faith could speak for the whole nation. But with that came a significant blind spot about how faith was defined by those who enjoyed less cultural influence. While civil religion can no longer unify the nation today, we're not sure it ever worked as well as Bellah and others believed. Only 8% of the population may have been something other than Christian when he wrote his piece, but that doesn't mean they didn't count. Were there times when they felt marginalized as second-class citizens because of the way civil religion was accepted as innocent and perceived as inclusive and unifying? What if civil religion was never as harmless as generations of scholars have suggested?

Interestingly, Bellah himself highlighted a key area where civil religion seemed to crack. In doing so, he drew attention to why it is untenable in an increasingly pluralistic and religiously unaffiliated nation: "We have had a Catholic president; it is conceivable that we could have a Jewish one. But could we have an agnostic president? Could a man with conscientious scruples about using the word God the way Kennedy and Johnson have used it be elected chief magistrate of our country?"[22] That is indeed an important question. And more than five decades later it seems he may have been too optimistic about America's civil religious future. We still don't have

---

[21] Bellah, "Civil Religion," 1967, 4.
[22] Bellah, "Civil Religion," 1967, 15.

a Jewish president. And not only have all our presidents since then professed to be Christian, but they also don't talk about God "the way Kennedy and Johnson" did. Instead, our presidents talk about God more frequently, are more explicitly Christian and sectarian in their religious-political appeals, and are even more partisan with such God-talk.[23] Largely gone are the days of civil religious presidential rhetoric. With this shift, we are heading closer to the world Bellah predicted would arise "if the whole God symbolism requires reformulation."[24] He argued, "There will be obvious consequences for the civil religion, consequences perhaps of liberal alienation and of fundamentalist ossification." Those words from the past seem to aptly describe the present.

While civil religion is an important sociological concept, civil religion wasn't as innocent as it seemed a few decades ago. Additionally, some things labeled as "civil religion" actually became the cornerstones laid for the Christian Nationalism dividing our churches and our country. Moreover, the increasing religious pluralism in the United States makes the assumptions undergirding civil religions far less plausible. The tradition that Bellah and others identified may have been less dangerous than Christian Nationalism in an earlier era, but its disintegration may also be far less of a loss than some would imagine given the religious demographics and political challenges of our contemporary moment.

Civil Religion's Agnosticism

There are other reasons to be quite skeptical of civil religion. The obvious one is the theology (or lack thereof) that it promotes. The concept trades on ambiguity as the words and symbols it employs are not clearly delineated. This allows (nearly) everyone to be included because there is no common interpretation of the national dogma. But to believe in something is to care about the details and the nuances. Christians debate and disagree—and divide—precisely because the content of their faith matters. Civil religion depends on downplaying differences in ways that empty religious affirmations of their meaning. In a profound way, to participate in civil religion requires the denial of one's true faith.

[23] Kaylor, *Presidential Campaign Rhetoric in an Age of Confessional Politics.*
[24] Bellah, "Civil Religion," 1967, 15.

Christian writer and editor Rodney Clapp illuminated this dynamic well in a 2004 article for *The Christian Century* titled, "The Problem with 'Under God.'"[25] Examining the ideas and arguments in a case before the Supreme Court about the constitutionality of the words "under God" in the Pledge of Allegiance, Clapp reached the conclusion that "the 'God' Americans are to pledge their nation to be 'under' is at worst an idol and at best the true God's name taken in vain." He reached that conclusion based on several statements made by some of the justices themselves. For example, Chief Justice William Rehnquist denied that saying the Pledge constitutes a "religious exercise" and that reciting "'under God' is in no sense a prayer, nor an endorsement of any religion." Instead, Rehnquist argued that those making the oath "promise fidelity to our flag and our nation, not to any particular God, faith, or church." Similarly, Justice Sandra Day O'Connor dismissed the phrase as "ceremonial deism" and claimed it was a "simple reference to a generic 'God.'"[26]

The reason the language of civil religion passes constitutional muster, at least according to these two justices, is that it is not actually religious at all. It's only because the name "God" means so little that the vague reference to an unspecified deity can remain in the Pledge of Allegiance. Whether or not this logic holds up in a pluralist democracy, it should not carry much weight with those who proclaim Jesus to be Lord. As Clapp argued, those defending the inclusion of "under God" in the Pledge—an issue we'll look at in depth in chapter 5—justify their position by "expressly denying that the God here referred to is the God of Israel, met in Jesus Christ. And they can do so only by admitting outright that for such a pledge they want an amorphous 'God' who is always and only on the side of the flag and the Republic for which it stands."

All this shows the inherent difficulty of civil religion. To be truly unifying, it must be intentionally vague in ways that sap language, symbols, and ideas of their meaning. Assigning meaning to its concepts involves excluding people who cannot religiously or intellectually embrace the more specific claims. For Christians and adherents of other faith traditions, civil religion risks becoming a

---

[25] Rodney Clapp, "The Problem with 'Under God,'" *The Christian Century*, November 16, 2004, https://www.religion-online.org/article/the-problem-with-under-god.

[26] Clapp, "The Problem with 'Under God.'"

mockery of their faith. It employs what they hold to be sacred in ways that run the danger of transforming their most cherished practices and deepest held beliefs into something profane. The civil religious "god" might have unified the nation, but to what good? As Johnson asked in his 1965 voting rights speech before Congress: "What is a man profited, if he shall gain the whole world, and lose his own soul?"

Section II

HOW MAINLINE PROTESTANTS BROUGHT CHURCH TO STATE

Chapter 4

PRAYER TIME

On the afternoon of January 6, 2021, as congressional members hid from the MAGA mob running through the Capitol hallways, some of the insurrectionists made their way into the Senate Chamber. Luke Mogelson of *The New Yorker* captured video as rioters sorted through desks and papers in a quest for some sort of "evidence" of wrongdoing.[1] Then in walked Jacob Chansley, nicknamed the "QAnon Shaman" for spouting conspiracy theories while wearing face paint and a fur hat with horns. After dropping a couple of f-bombs, he saw a guy with blood on himself and said, "Look at this guy. He's covered in blood. God bless you." A badly-outnumbered police officer asked them to leave the Senate Chamber because "this is like the sacrediest place." The insurrectionists ignored his plea and instead lined up behind the podium.

"Jesus Christ, we invoke your name! Amen!" one of them shouted with a hand raised upward.

Others also shouted "amen" as Chansley, suddenly inspired, added, "Let's all say a prayer in this sacred space." He set down the American flag he'd been carrying and picked up a bullhorn to pray. He started, paused for everyone to take off their Trump hats (or furry horns), and then started again:

Thank you, heavenly Father, for this opportunity to stand up for God-given unalienable rights. Thank you, heavenly Father, for being the inspiration needed to these police

---

[1] "A Reporter's Footage from Inside the Capitol Siege," *The New Yorker*, January 17, 2021, https://www.newyorker.com/news/video-dept/a-reporters-footage-from-inside-the-capitol-siege.

officers to allow us into the building, to allow us to exercise our rights, to allow us to send a message to all the tyrants, the communists, and the globalists that this is our nation, not theirs. ...Thank you, divine, omniscient, omnipotent, and omnipresent Creator God, for filling this chamber with your white light of love, your white light of harmony. Thank you for filling this chamber with patriots that love you and that love Christ. ... Thank you for allowing the United States of America to be reborn. Thank you for allowing us to get rid of the communists, the globalists, and the traitors within our government. We love you and we thank you. In Christ's holy name we pray. Amen!

That prayer quickly became a key exhibit in understanding the Christian Nationalism that helped fuel the attack on the Capitol. Chansley was arrested and sentenced to 41 months in prison (not for the theological crime of the prayer but for the actions that had gotten him to that spot). Yet, the QAnon Shaman wasn't the first person to petition God from the Senate podium on January 6. Someone else had been paid by U.S. taxpayers to pray there.

"Almighty God, have compassion on us with your unfailing love," Senate Chaplain Barry Black, a Seventh-day Adventist, offered just after the Senate was called to order at 12:30 p.m.[2]

As he often does with his prayers, the chaplain included political references and even took sides in an ongoing political debate—in this case, the opposite side of the insurrectionist prayer that would come from that spot a couple of hours later. But the differences aren't quite so black and white. While literally praying for the opposite outcome, Black and those backing Trump both prayed for the vote and wise decisions by lawmakers. Black prayed:

As our lawmakers prepare to formally certify the votes cast by the electoral college, be present with them. Guide our legislators with your wisdom and truth as they seek to meet the requirements of the U.S. Constitution. Lord, inspire them to seize this opportunity to demonstrate to the nation and world how the democratic process can be done properly and in an orderly manner. Help them to remember that history

---

[2] *United States of America Congressional Record, Proceedings and Debates of the 117th Congress, First Session* 167 (2021): S13.

is a faithful stenographer, and so are you. We pray in your sovereign name. Amen.

After listening to those words, the senators started the process to certify the election.

Prayers like that from the government's podium occur as part of the nation's official discourse and are included word for word in the *Congressional Record*. And they're uttered by someone elected by congressional leaders and whose salary is paid for by U.S. taxpayers. They also matter as public communication because even though the prayers address God, the members of Congress are clearly an intended audience (as well as nerds like us watching C-SPAN 2). As one of us (Brian) argued in the book *Sacramental Politics* after analyzing Black's prayers during the 2013 government shutdown, "Clearly it cannot be cast as merely a spiritual encounter with the divine given its political resonance, nor can it be stripped of its sacredness to be situated as merely political rhetoric."[3] Which is more representative of Christian Nationalism: a man breaking into the building one day to offer one prayer, or an ordained Christian minister standing there each day with the authority of the government to pray on behalf of the nation?

Across the Capitol on January 6, Black's House colleague, Rev. Margaret Kibben, had a few minutes earlier also given an official government prayer as lawmakers listened. Like her counterpart, the Presbyterian Church (U.S.A.) minister took sides in the societal debate literally brewing on the steps and about to burst in—and even criticized some congressional members with her words.

"We who have pledged to defend our Constitution against all enemies, we pray your hedge of protection around this nation," she said. "Defend us from those adversaries, both foreign and domestic, outside these walls and perhaps within these Chambers, who sow seeds of acrimony to divide colleagues and conspire to undermine trust in your divine authority over all things."[4]

Although speaking on behalf of a chamber that includes members from various faiths or who claim no faith at all, Kibben—

---

[3] Brian Kaylor, *Sacramental Politics: Religious Worship as Political Action* (New York: Peter Lang Publishing), 79.

[4] *United States of America Congressional Record, Proceedings and Debates of the 117th Congress, First Session* 167 (2021): H75.

like Black—prayed as if speaking for the entire gathered assembly of lawmakers. Part of her prayer even suggested nonbelievers aren't wise, and she advanced the narrative of a divine plan for the nation.

"The journey of this experiment in democracy is perilous and demanding, fraught with anger and discontent. But wise rulers still seek you," she prayed. "So help us, God, to find you in the midst of us. So help us, God, to see your gracious plan even in the events of these days."

In her prayer, Kibben asked for God to help the lawmakers "serve you and this nation." She also prayed that in "our deliberations and our debates" that God "would be revealed and exalted among the nations." Praying on just her third day on the job, Kibben baptized the formal work of the government as she asked for God to help the legislators serve God so that God "would be revealed and exalted among the people." She wore a mask instead of face paint and a pastoral collar instead of a furry hat, but her presence and practice still depicted the U.S. as a Christian nation.

Several hours later—early on the morning of January 7 after the insurrection had been put down and the presidential votes officially certified—Black voiced a prayer to end the joint congressional session. In his prayer, he continued the tradition of using the "we" to speak on behalf of Congress and even the nation. He declared that "we deplore the desecration of the United States Capitol Building, the shedding of innocent blood, the loss of life, and the quagmire of dysfunction that threaten our democracy."[5] While some lawmakers disagreed with his assessment of the vote, others don't accept his faith assertions made on behalf of the entire nation. He added:

> You have strengthened our resolve to protect and defend the Constitution of the United States against all enemies domestic, as well as foreign. ... Thank you for what you have blessed our lawmakers to accomplish in spite of threats to liberty. Bless and keep us. Drive far from us all wrong desires, incline our hearts to do your will, and guide our feet on the path of peace. And God bless America.

A few seconds later, Vice President Mike Pence ended the joint session that, by confirming his ticket's loss, answered some of the

---

[5] *United States of America Congressional Record, Proceedings and Debates of the 117th Congress, First Session* 167 (2021): H115.

prayers uttered in that chamber and denied others. And while the QAnon Shaman later went to prison for his behavior, the chaplains returned day after day to offer official government prayers. Christian Nationalism in the Capitol didn't end on January 6. And mainline Protestants created this daily display of the ideology.

While Kibben and Black use inclusive language in their prayers, they are still ordained ministers using Christian language to perform a sectarian spiritual practice—all while speaking on behalf of the U.S. Congress. That's why James Madison and some clergy during the founding period of the U.S. argued against congressional chaplains as a problematic establishment of religion.[6] Madison won a lot of debates on church-state separation, but not that one. Thus, we've had chaplains since the beginning of Congress, with the jobs largely going to mainline Protestants.

Although Kibben is the first woman to serve as a congressional chaplain, her denominational affiliation is more mundane. Her two immediate predecessors were the only Catholics to serve as House chaplains, but before that Presbyterians and other mainline Protestants—like Methodists and American Baptists—dominated the list. The first session of Congress saw newly-elected members heading to New York in March 1789. After a quorum was achieved in the House of Representatives on April 1, they elected a speaker and got to work. One month later, the members elected Rev. William Linn, a Presbyterian minister, as the first chaplain. The next two were also Presbyterians. And among the 53 House chaplains, 16 have been Methodists (30%), 15 Presbyterians (28%), 7 American Baptists (13%), and 4 Episcopalians (8%). That's 79% from just four traditions. There were also two each among the Lutherans, Disciples of Christ, and Congregationalists (a key branch of today's United Church of Christ). That just leaves two Catholics and three Unitarians or Universalists.

A similar story exists in the Senate. Although the current chaplain, Barry Black, is the first Seventh-day Adventist to serve, he followed three Presbyterian Church (U.S.A.) pastors who held that job in succession from 1969 until 2003. Episcopalians and Methodists often filled that role before then. Not only was the original Senate

[6] Brian Kaylor, "The Democratic Sin of Congressional Chaplains," *Roll Call*, January 5, 2021, https://rollcall.com/2021/01/05/the-democratic-sin-of-congressional-chaplains.

chaplain an Episcopalian, but the first six people in this position were, thus putting the denomination birthed out of the state church of England in charge of official Senate payers for the first 18 years. Of the 52 people who've served as a Senate chaplain, 16 have been Episcopalians (30%), 13 Presbyterians (25%), 12 Methodists (23%), and 5 American Baptists (10%). That's 88% from just four traditions, the same four traditions that also dominate the House chaplains list. The six other Senate chaplains are two Unitarians, a Lutheran, a Congregationalist, a Catholic, and the current Seventh-day Adventist.

Since seven people served as a chaplain in both houses at some point, that leaves us with a total of 98 different people as a House or Senate chaplain in over 230 years. Methodists have led the way with 26 (27%), followed by Presbyterians with 24 (24%), Episcopalians with 20 (20%), and American Baptists with 11 (11%). Once again, just four traditions have provided 83% of the congressional chaplains. Other mainline denominations (or precursor traditions) have accounted for another 8%, leaving just 9% from Catholics, Seventh-day Adventists, Unitarians, and Universalists. That means many significant Christian denominations and traditions have not yet been chosen to send a congressional chaplain, nor have non-Christian religious traditions. When congressional members have bowed their heads for official prayers, it's usually been with a mainline minister standing at the podium. Christian Nationalistic prayers didn't just come into the Capitol during the insurrection; mainline clergy first spent two centuries regularly baptizing America's leaders as instruments of God.

Light of Dwight

On January 20, 1953, Dwight D. Eisenhower placed his hand on two Bibles to take the presidential oath of office for the first time.[7] One Bible had been used by George Washington for the oath in 1789 and was opened to 2 Chronicles 7:14 (and presumably other verses around it)—"If my people, which are called by my name, shall humble themselves, and pray, and seek my face, and turn from their wicked ways; then will I hear from heaven, and will forgive their sin, and will heal their land." The other holy book was his "West Point Bible"

---

[7] "42nd Inaugural Ceremonies," Joint Congressional Committee on Inaugural Ceremonies, January 20, 1953, https://www.inaugural.senate. gov/42nd-inaugural-ceremonies.

open to Psalm 33:12—"Blessed is the nation whose God is the Lord; and the people whom he hath chosen for his own inheritance." After taking the oath, Eisenhower looked out over the crowd and said that before giving some remarks, he would be "uttering a little private prayer of my own." But it wasn't actually private and he requested the nation to join him: "I ask that you bow your heads." He then prayed aloud:

> Almighty God, as we stand here at this moment, my future associates in the Executive Branch of government join me in beseeching that thou will make full and complete our dedication to the service of the people in this throng, and their fellow citizens everywhere. ... May cooperation be permitted and be the mutual aim of those who, under the concepts of our Constitution, hold to differing political faiths; so that all may work for the good of our beloved country and thy glory. Amen.[8]

Having christened the executive branch to work for God's glory, he then offered his inaugural address. He would soon continue to find other ways of consecrating his administration as God's servants. But first, he would decide to baptize the presidency in a more literal way. Although Eisenhower grew up in a devout family, he had never joined a church. His military service marked a sharp departure from the pacifist faith of his family. Initially, his parents had been part of the River Brethren (an Anabaptist group that split off from the Mennonites) and then became active with the Jehovah's Witnesses. As a child, Eisenhower attended with his parents but never committed to either group.

As Ike launched his political career, he decided to officially align with the Presbyterian tradition of his wife. He attended a prayer service on the morning of his inauguration in 1953 at National Presbyterian Church. It is the national congregation of what is today known as the Presbyterian Church (U.S.A.). President Harry Truman previously attended the consecration service when it received this denominational status (and Eisenhower later laid the cornerstone for a new building). Four of the congregation's pastors have served as Senate chaplains. Several presidents attended and there's even

---

[8] Dwight D. Eisenhower, "Inaugural Address," January 20, 1953, https://www.presidency.ucsb.edu/documents/inaugural-address-3.

"The President's Pew" in the church. They also have a "Chapel of the Presidents" that includes stained-glass windows of presidents George Washington, Abraham Lincoln, Teddy Roosevelt, Woodrow Wilson, Franklin D. Roosevelt, and Eisenhower—and since other than Ike those presidents were not part of that congregation, they were clearly chosen because of their national prominence or other criteria over their religious connection. For Eisenhower, the window portrays him signing the bill adding "under God" to the Pledge of Allegiance (more on that issue in chapter 5).

Twelve days after the inaugural prayer gathering at National City Presbyterian, Eisenhower returned. This time to be baptized and join the church in a special gathering with Rev. Edward L.R. Elson before the Sunday service on February 1, 1953. Elson, who would later serve as a Senate chaplain from 1969–1981, had led the church since 1946. He had already developed relationships with significant politicians—and sometimes publicized it. In 1950, he wrote a piece for *The Chaplain* magazine titled "The J. Edgar Hoover You Ought to Know, by His Pastor" that praised the godliness of the FBI director. Hoover later wrote the introduction to Elson's book *America's Spiritual Recovery*, which Elson dedicated to then-President Eisenhower for "giving testimony to the reality of America's spiritual foundation." (Hoover, a lifelong Presbyterian, also helped contribute to Christian Nationalism in numerous other ways.[9]) In Elson's book, the pastor argued America was founded upon a faith in God and that democracy requires Christianity. He later shared more stories of his interactions with Truman, Eisenhower, Kennedy, and many others (including Queen Elizabeth II) in his autobiography *Wide Was His Parish*. Elson had met Eisenhower years earlier as a military chaplain, and the general asked Elson at the close of World War II to represent him before a body that was considering how to rebuild the German Protestant Church that had been Nazified.

Several years after dealing with a state church in Germany, Elson brought a state leader under the baptismal waters. As Elson later recalled, Eisenhower came to the church for a special baptism ceremony witnessed by most of the congregation's elders (instead of doing it before the whole church during the service an

---

[9] Lerone A. Martin, *The Gospel of J. Edgar Hoover: How the FBI Aided and Abetted the Rise of White Christian Nationalism* (Princeton: Princeton University Press, 2023).

hour later). Elson baptized the new president, the elders received both Eisenhowers into membership, and they were announced as new members before communion during the regular service. That development quickly sparked headlines across the country. As Elson recalled, "Nothing like this had happened before in American history. Later, a historian on the faculty of the Catholic University in America telephoned me to say that the baptism of the president must be the first baptism of a chief of state since Clovis I, king of the Franks in the sixth century."[10] According to Elson, his pastoral advice also sometimes covered domestic and foreign policy issues the president was addressing.

As we'll see throughout this section, the Eisenhower years saw a zeal for Christian Nationalism. Elson watched up close many of the developments we highlight in this and the next two chapters, but he offered a more affirmative opinion than we do. In his autobiography, he wrote about his famous late parishioner's prayer at his inaugural address and connected that to what he saw happen over the next eight years: "[The prayer] symbolized an emphasis during the entire presidency that followed. The decade of the 1950s was characterized by a marked upsurge in religious faith and spiritual renewal. The president, by his attitude, his words, and his practice, became a model of the spiritual resurgence in the nation."[11] Hoover, in his introduction for Elson's earlier book, also praised Eisenhower's inaugural prayer and presidency for representing a nation returning to God. But what some saw as a spiritual resurgence looks in hindsight like the building of Christian Nationalism.

National Prayer (Along with Breakfast)

Four days after Eisenhower's baptism, another key effort was launched to promote prayer and Jesus in the government: the National Prayer Breakfast. The key figure behind the creation of the National Prayer Breakfast was Kansas Republican Sen. Frank Carlson,[12] an American Baptist layman who served as chair of the National Prayer Breakfast for its first 17 years. He was also a

[10] Edward L. R. Elson, *Wide Was His Parish* (Wheaton: Tyndale House Publishers, 1986), 117–118.
[11] Elson, *Wide Was His Parish*, 113.
[12] Kevin M. Kruse, *One Nation Under God: How Corporate America Invented Christian America* (New York: Basic Books, 2015).

speaker at the first one (along with Eisenhower) and again in 1959 and 1967. Carlson had been participating in private Senate prayer breakfasts and invited Eisenhower to one after his fellow Kansan won the presidency. When word got out that the new president would attend, it quickly became obvious the normal meeting spot wouldn't work. So Carlson got Conrad Hilton, a Catholic, to host it at a hotel. That first event in 1953 was held with the theme of "Government Under God." Eisenhower's presence—along with members of Congress and the U.S. Supreme Court—gave this breakfast sponsored by the International Council for Christian Leadership the appearance of an official event. Republican Rep. Katharine St. George, an Episcopalian from New York, opened the event with prayer and Scripture reading.

"Bless, we pray thee, this thy servant, the president of the United States, the members of his Cabinet, the Congress, and all of our people. Give us wisdom and strength to do thy will. We know that if thou are for us, none can be against us," St. George prayed. "We do not ask these things trusting in our own righteousness, but in thy mercy and the love of our savior, Jesus Christ."[13]

St. George then led the gathered congregation of politicos in saying the Lord's Prayer, the text of which Carlson put in the *Congressional Record* as part of the full transcript of the event (in case you were wondering, they prayed to forgive trespasses, not debts).

Before inviting Eisenhower to the podium, Carlson offered a few remarks. Noting the event's theme, he read a biblical passage where the prophet Samuel declared about the ancient Hebrew people, "Hitherto, hath the Lord helped us." Carlson argued "that can be truly said of our nation."[14]

"This occasion is to me in truth a landmark in our government," Carlson added. "From the quietness and simplicity of such meetings as this, in Christ's name and with his spirit, there comes to men an inner structure. It is our prayer that armed with this inner strength you, Dwight D. Eisenhower, may mount up with the wings of an eagle, may run and not be weary, may walk and not faint."[15]

---

[13] *United States of America Congressional Record, Proceedings and Debates of the 83rd Congress, Second Session, Appendix* 99 (1953): A571.
[14] *United States of America Congressional Record,* A572.
[15] *United States of America Congressional Record,* A572–A573.

Eisenhower then rose to confer his official blessing on the event. His presence—and that of his successors—adds to the event sometimes being erroneously referred to as the "President's Prayer Breakfast" even though it has been run by a nongovernmental Christian organization with the participation of members of the legislative and executive branches.

"The very basis of our government is: We hold 'that all men are endowed by their Creator' with certain rights," Eisenhower said in his remarks. "In one sentence we established that every free government is embedded soundly in a deeply-felt religious faith or it makes no sense."[16]

Rev. Edward Pruden, pastor of First Baptist Church in Washington, D.C., closed the National Prayer Breakfast in prayer. A recent president of the American Baptist Convention, Pruden had served as Harry Truman's pastor for most of Truman's presidency (Truman stopped attending in 1951 after Pruden publicly criticized the president's nomination of a government emissary to the Holy See). During his National Prayer Breakfast prayer, Pruden quoted from Psalm 33 that "happy is the nation whose God is the Lord." He added, "And to those words we would add our own words, 'Happy is the nation whose leaders recognize and honor God.'"[17] Like others, he closed his prayer by invoking "our Lord Jesus Christ."

After the event, Senate Chaplain Frederick Brown Harris, a Methodist minister, gushed in a column for the *Washington Star* (which Carlson added to the *Congressional Record*) that the event was "one of the most amazing prayer meetings ever held since Washington agonized on the frozen ground of Valley Forge."[18] Praising both Eisenhower's inaugural day prayer and the prayer breakfast, Harris called them signs of "the new under-God consciousness which is gripping our leaders."

"The Return-to-God movement is more than a slogan. It is assuming the proportions of a holy crusade," he wrote. "In a twentieth century Declaration of Dependence—on God—is America on its knees. And on its knees America is invincible."

---

[16] Dwight D. Eisenhower, "Remarks at the Dedicatory Prayer Breakfast of the International Christian Leadership," February 5, 1953, https://www.presidency.ucsb.edu/documents/remarks-the-dedicatory-prayer-breakfast-the-international-christian-leadership.

[17] *United States of America Congressional Record*, A573.

[18] *United States of America Congressional Record*, A655–A656.

Another key National Prayer Breakfast organizer was Abraham Vereide, a Methodist minister. At the inaugural 1953 event, Vereide led a "prayer of consecration" for Eisenhower. He thanked God that Eisenhower and the others had been chosen to lead the nation and prayed that God would guide the governmental officials to follow God's guidance and word. He closed the prayer with a clear sectarian tone: "We thank thee, our Father, for hearing us and accepting us, for Jesus's sake and in his name. Amen."[19]

Vereide was not a stranger in that room, having set the stage for such a high-powered breakfast over the previous couple of decades. In 1935, Vereide created the International Council for Christian Leadership, later known as The Fellowship Foundation (aka "The Family") to lead prayer breakfasts across the country. Carlson was already involved with Vereide's work before getting Eisenhower to show up to launch the National Prayer Breakfast. For more than a decade before that, Vereide mingled with members of Congress, Supreme Court justices, Cabinet members, and other political leaders who attended the prayer gatherings of his group.

In addition to weekly prayer gatherings for House and Senate members, he also put together special sessions. Like when Fred Vinson, a member of a Methodist Episcopal church, became the Chief Justice in 1946. After an introduction by the U.S. attorney general, Vinson addressed the prayer gathering for senators (who had just confirmed him). According to Vereide's authorized biographer and confidante, Vinson gave his testimony and "emphasized the importance of the Bible being the book of all people and how the whole superstructure of government and jurisprudence is built upon it."[20] Then the 28 senators at the event joined a prayer of dedication for the new chief justice. Missouri Republican Sen. Forrest Donnell, who had taught Sunday School classes and had been active in Methodist life in Missouri, gave the prayer "dedicating [Vinson] in the name of the Father, the Son, and the Holy Spirit to his exalted and important position."

The day after the first National Prayer Breakfast in 1953, an apparently inspired Eisenhower started the practice of opening

---

[19] *United States of America Congressional Record*, A572.

[20] Norman Grubb, *Modern Viking: The Story of Abraham Vereide, Pioneer in Christian Leadership* (Grand Rapids: Zondervan Publishing House, 1961), 111.

his Cabinet meetings with prayer. Carlson and the other organizers found the breakfast so successful that it quickly became an annual effort. The next year, Carlson told the crowd they had gathered "to renew our faith and commitment in God."[21] U.S. Rep. Charles Bennett of Florida, a member of a Disciples of Christ congregation and the key sponsor a couple of years later to put "In God We Trust" on currency (more on that issue in chapter 6), opened the event in prayer. And Chief Justice Earl Warren, who was raised Methodist but was identified at the time as part of an American Baptist church, insisted that "no one can read the history of our country without realizing that the Good Book and the spirit of the Savior have from the beginning been our guiding geniuses."[22] He argued the colonial founders had a clear objective: "a Christian land governed by Christian principles." Thus, he added, "We are a Christian nation."[23] In 1961, newly-inaugurated President John F. Kennedy spoke at the National Prayer Breakfast, helping secure its legacy as it moved into a new administration and with a president and vice president of the other party attending and speaking. That year the organization also expanded with the launch of a simultaneous "Congressional Wives' Prayer Breakfast." At Carlson's request, Kennedy popped into that gathering to offer a few remarks.

Vereide's group was later led by Presbyterian minister Richard Halverson (who became Senate chaplain while leading the National Prayer Breakfast group) and Doug Coe (an ordained Presbyterian Church (U.S.A.) elder). The group became the key force organizing and raising funds for the National Prayer Breakfast over the seven decades that followed. Coe also built strong ties with politicians in Congress and other nations, often engaging in international diplomacy along the way. The influence of Coe and The Family has been well-documented by journalist Jeff Sharlet in his book *The Family: The Secret Fundamentalism at the Heart of American Power* (which led to the Netflix documentary series *The Family*). With those big-name speakers and large crowds of influential politicians, the National Prayer Breakfast quickly became a "who's who" of Washington. And with that came opportunities to influence

---

[21] "Breakfast in Washington," *Time*, February 15, 1954, https://content.time.com/time/subscriber/article/0,33009,936197,00.html.

[22] "Breakfast in Washington."

[23] Kruse, *One Nation Under God*, 80.

public policy. Politicking often comes as a side along with the coffee and muffins.

It hasn't just been domestic deals at the breakfast as the event grew to include large delegations of international representatives— including an alleged Russian spy. As a result of the Mueller special counsel investigation into ties between Russian and Trump officials, a few dozen people were charged with crimes (with most of those in the U.S. pleading guilty or being convicted). Prosecutors referred several individuals to other agencies, including alleged Russian spy Maria Butina. After her arrest by the FBI, she pleaded guilty, served an 18-month prison sentence, and was deported back to Russia (where she was then elected to the Russian legislature as part of Vladimir Putin's ruling party). Among other activities, the U.S. Justice Department's affidavit accused Butina of attempting to use the 2017 National Prayer Breakfast as part of her effort to "establish a back channel of communication" between Russian and U.S. officials.[24] As she corresponded with National Prayer Breakfast organizers, she noted that Russian attendees to the event were "important political advisors" to Putin. And she saw the event as critical for relations between Putin and Trump, writing, "A new relationship between two countries always begins better when it begins in faith."

Then came the 2020 National Prayer Breakfast. The day before it occurred, the U.S. Senate had voted to acquit Trump in his first impeachment (the one prompted by Trump's attempt to get a personal political favor done by shaking down Ukrainian president Volodymyr Zelensky—who later led Ukraine to stand up to Putin's aggression). Trump waltzed onto the stage holding up copies of newspapers with the headline "Trump Acquitted." And the crowd responded with applause, not prayer. At an event that organizers insist brings people together across party lines, Trump instead lobbed partisan attacks. Not only did he go after his political opponents as "very corrupt and dishonest people," but he also attacked their faith.

"I don't like people who use faith for justification for doing what they know is wrong, nor do I like people who say 'I pray for you'

[24] Jack Jenkins, "Mariia Butina and the National Prayer Breakfast," *Religion News Service*, July 18, 2018, https://religionnews.com/2018/07/18/why-mariia-butina-wasnt-the-only-russian-targeting-the-national-prayer-breakfast.

when they know that is not so," said Trump,[25] apparently confusing praying for someone with supporting them politically.

While the attacks were bipartisan—he questioned the faith of both Democratic Speaker of the House Nancy Pelosi and Republican Sen. Mitt Romney—it represented the opposite of what National Prayer Breakfast organizers claim the event is about. But it's all part of the world mainline Protestant leaders helped create where a quasi-official event featuring the president and members of Congress occurs every year to declare that the U.S. government should be built on a Christian foundation. As Amanda Tyler of the Baptist Joint Committee for Religious Liberty explained:

> Even though this isn't a government-sponsored event, the optics of it make it look and feel official and make it look like the government is sponsoring the event. ... Having this private event sponsored by an explicitly Christian organization, and having all of these indicators that the government is heavily involved, sends this signal to people watching that to be truly welcome—certainly in this room and overall in America—that one has to be Christian.[26]

Congressional leaders created a new nonprofit to take over control of the event from The Family in 2023 after the controversies of the Trump years, thus making the event even more official. And in 2024, it moved into the Capitol for the first time after Speaker Mike Johnson opened up Statuary Hall for the event. All in the name of Jesus. As Democratic Sen. Chris Coons of Delaware, a Presbyterian who studied at Yale Divinity School, explained in defense of the National Prayer Breakfast in 2022, it's a time for U.S. leaders to "come together in a nonsectarian celebration of prayer in the spirit of Jesus."[27] We quibble with his definition of "nonsectarian"

[25] David Crary, "Trump's Prayer Breakfast Jibes Jolt Many Faith Leaders," *Associated Press*, February 6, 2020, https://apnews.com/article/b971362e7b56d77dd59f3a973ff916a6.

[26] Jeff Brumley, "National Prayer Breakfast Gets New Sponsorship But Still Looks Like Government-Sponsored Religion, BJC Leaders Say," *Baptist News Global*, January 31, 2023, https://baptistnews.com/article/national-prayer-breakfast-gets-new-sponsorship-but-still-looks-like-government-sponsored-religion-bjc-leaders-say.

[27] Jack Jenkins, "Sen. Chris Coons: This year's National Prayer Breakfast is a 'Reset,'" *Religion News Service*, February 2, 2022, https://religionnews.com/2022/02/02/sen-chris-coons-this-years-national-prayer-breakfast-is-a-reset.

as he frames the event like the founders and speakers at the first breakfasts did: in the name of Jesus. Thus, each February the National Prayer Breakfast presents a clear Christian Nationalistic image to the country, suggesting a connection between the prosperity of our country and our elected leaders' commitment to Jesus.

Chapter 5

ONE NATION ... INDIVISIBLE

"The Democrats took the word God out of the Pledge of Allegiance at the Democrat[ic] National Convention."[1] That's the false claim then-President Donald Trump made on Twitter in August 2020 after his opponent Joe Biden officially accepted the Democratic nomination for president. But while the DNC did include the phrase "under God" in the Pledge for each night's session, the Baptist minister credited with writing the Pledge left God out of it.

Trump made his claim, which he repeated during his acceptance remarks at the Republican National Convention, because two DNC virtual caucus gatherings—those of the LGBTQ Caucus and the Muslim Delegates and Allies Assembly—had included recitations of the Pledge without "under God." But each of the main DNC evening sessions—the carefully scripted televised programs during the week of meetings—included the phrase in the Pledge. On the night Biden gave his acceptance address, his five eldest grandchildren led the gathered delegates in the Pledge and said "under God." Biden himself also invoked the phrase in his remarks.

"With passion and purpose, let us begin—you and I together, one nation under God—united in our love for America and united in our love for each other," Biden declared.[2]

The political charge of leaving out "under God" pops up regularly in our ongoing culture wars. To suggest the removal of "God" from the

---

[1] Donald J. Trump (@realDonaldTrump), August 22, 2020, https://twitter.com/realDonaldTrump/status/1297132096448864258.

[2] "Transcript: Joe Biden's DNC Speech," August 21, 2020, https://www.cnn.com/2020/08/20/politics/biden-dnc-speech-transcript/index.html.

Pledge is to commit an unforgivable political sin. Rev. Brenda Bartella Peterson learned that the hard way in 2004. An ordained minister in the Christian Church (Disciples of Christ), she briefly served as the religious advisor for the Democratic National Committee leading up to the convention that nominated John Kerry. But she resigned after facing public attacks for being one of 32 Christian and Jewish clergy members who signed an amicus curiae brief with the U.S. Supreme Court supporting a suit challenging the constitutionality of "under God" in the Pledge. Sixteen years later, Trump recognized such an issue could still resonate. But while Biden and other Democrats said "under God," the man long credited with writing the Pledge in 1892 left it out.[3] And 'God' would stay out of it for another 62 years—until mainline Protestants pledged to change our nation's oath.

The son of a Baptist minister in New York, Francis Bellamy followed in his father's vocational footsteps. The younger Bellamy attended Rochester Theological Seminary (now known as Colgate Rochester Crozer Divinity School, which is affiliated with American Baptist Churches USA), and he pastored Baptist churches in New York and Massachusetts. He also wrote for a number of publications, including the children's magazine *The Youth's Companion*.

For the 400th anniversary of Christopher Columbus reaching the Americas, the 37-year-old Bellamy wrote a salute to the U.S. flag to be used for Columbus Day celebrations. Since *The Youth's Companion* funded itself in part by selling American flags, pushing a patriotic salute was good for business. The September 8, 1892, issue carried Bellamy's recommended oath: "I pledge allegiance to my Flag and the Republic for which it stands, one nation, indivisible, with liberty and justice for all." As his words grew in use over the next few decades, the U.S. Congress officially recognized a slightly edited version in 1942: "I pledge allegiance to the flag of the United States of America, and to the Republic for which it stands, one Nation indivisible, with liberty and justice for all." Still no "God." Just as Bellamy intended.

---

[3] Although Francis Bellamy has historically been credited as the author of the Pledge of Allegiance, new evidence in 2022 questions that story. But at the time Trump made his remarks, Bellamy was the believed author. For more about the conflicting claims, see Sam Roberts, "We Know the Pledge. Its Author, Maybe Not," *New York Times*, April 2, 2022, https://www.nytimes.com/2022/04/02/us/pledge-of-allegiance-francis-bellamy.html.

The absence of "under God" in the Pledge isn't the only thing about Bellamy that would spark a political rant today. While Trump likes to label his Democratic opponents as "socialists," Bellamy actually was one. In fact, he started writing for *The Youth's Companion* after being pushed out of the pulpit at Bethany Baptist Church in Boston. The vice president of the Society of Christian Socialists, he discovered that not everyone appreciated his arguments about "Jesus the Socialist." In a piece in the May 1890 issue of the Society's newspaper, *The Dawn*, on advancing the cause of Christian socialism, he urged pastors to preach on socialistic themes—and even seemed to predict his own ministerial woes:

> The pastor, perhaps, cannot carry his congregation with him, should he avow himself a Christian Socialist; but he can preach frequently on themes having a decided bearing on the relation of Christ to current economics; and he can gather around him a select class of his acquaintances, from within and from without his church, who can study the questions of economics from the religious point of view.[4]

Later in that piece, he defined Christian socialism as "the science of the Golden Rule applied to economic relations."[5] But he noted it's difficult to advance since "the law of selfishness has been so thoroughly centered in the old and the current maxims of business," so they must "work in educating the public mind to right convictions on the place of righteousness in economics."

Trump probably wouldn't like that kind of preaching, just as he doesn't like the original Pledge. When he tweeted another critique of the DNC on a Sunday before he spent the morning golfing, he claimed the absence of "under God" from the Pledge at the two caucus meetings "sounded not only strange, but terrible."[6] Yet, for nearly half its life, that's exactly how the Pledge sounded. The story of how the Pledge found religion is one that involves a global Cold War with a socialist nation. And the preaching of mainline Protestants.

---

[4] Francis Bellamy, "Education Department," *The Dawn*, May 1890, 43.
[5] Bellamy, "Education Department," 44.
[6] Donald J. Trump (@realDonaldTrump), August 23, 2020, https://twitter.com/realDonaldTrump/status/1297521970813317121.

Prepare Ye the Way

The addition of "under God" to the Pledge didn't occur in a vacuum. Cultural forces helped push the mindset that such a revision was needed. Mainline Protestant leaders helped make the case for the addition, like with the founding meeting of the National Council of Churches in 1950. The ecumenical movement in the U.S. had led in 1908 to the creation of the Federal Council of Churches, a body that included the mainline Protestant traditions, several Black denominations, and others. In 1950, the Federal Council merged with other ecumenical groups to create the National Council of Churches. This even more robust effort at ecumenism launched with an inaugural meeting in Cleveland, Ohio, that drew more than 5,000 people. And what was the theme of the constituting convention of the NCC? "This Nation Under God." That emphasis was not a one-off decision. Not only did the NCC start with this focus, but NCC General Secretary Edwin Espy (an American Baptist) declared nearly two decades later: "The National Council has stood for this view from the beginning. Its first and continuing slogan is 'This Nation Under God.'"[7]

At the meeting in Cleveland, Rev. Ralph Sockman, a Methodist pastor in New York, gave an address on the theme. He explained they had drawn it from Abraham Lincoln's Gettysburg Address, noting with numerological zeal that they were meeting "four score and seven years" from when Lincoln gave the speech about the birth of the nation "four score and seven years" earlier.[8] Sockman added that "never more than now was it so imperative" to follow "the spirit of Lincoln" in declaring "this nation under God."

Sockman also invoked the faith of the Puritans: "In a very real sense, this land was to them, 'God's Country.'"[9] He recounted other saints of the American experiment, defending the faith of deist Thomas Jefferson and placing him alongside devout Christians like George Washington and John Marshall.

---

[7] *Triennial Report: The National Council of the Churches of Christ in the U.S.A., 1966–1969* (New York: National Council of the Churches of Christ in the United States, 1969), 21.

[8] *Christian Faith in Action; Commemorative Volume: The Founding of the National Council of the Churches of Christ in the United States of America* (New York: National Council of the Churches of Christ in the United States, 1951), 67.

[9] *Christian Faith in Action*, 68.

"The laws, the institutions, the ideals of America stem from the soil of belief in a sovereign God," Sockman said. "Much of its social ferment is the yeasty germination of the principles put by Jesus in the faith of our founders."[10]

He also listed some constitutional principles as proof that "our religious faith has grown an American way of life." But included in this list 15 years before the Civil Rights Act was the claim that anyone can "cast his secret ballot in a free election." More significantly, he contrasted "this nation under God" with the key Cold War adversary: "In competing with communism for the minds of millions, Christians ought to be learning what Christ has that the Kremlin lacks. The compassion of the cross has more power and appeal than the compulsions of the crescent and the sickle."[11] Stockman also tried to reconcile the idea of a "chosen" nation with the ecumenical theology underlying the NCC that believed all people were equal:

> We do not think of our fathers as a "chosen people" in the sense that they were the special favorites of a divine champion. God is no respecter of persons. But he is a respecter of principles. And our fathers, though not "chosen favorites," were a choosing people, whose choice of principles enabled God to use them as chosen seed. And when we look back at those who, in "this nation under God," have given us our heritage, we humbly and gratefully acknowledge "that they are the seed which the Lord hath blessed."[12]

The last phrase came from Isaiah 61, thus calling the U.S. a new Israel, divinely chosen by God.

The meeting included a service to officially constitute the NCC, with leaders from member bodies joining the liturgy to declare their support. There were also other times of worship during the four-day conference that was filled with speeches, committee meetings, exhibits, and more. Amid hymns, prayers, speeches, and responsive readings, a large banner hung over the cross behind the pulpit declaring "This Nation Under God." The U.S. flag stood in the hall, with the United Nations flag and the Christian flag on either side. While

---

[10] *Christian Faith in Action*, 69.

[11] *Christian Faith in Action*, 73.

[12] *Christian Faith in Action*, 69.

most of the hymns chosen for the event were classic religious songs with little or no nationalistic content, the program did include the popular patriotic hymn "America the Beautiful," along with "God of Our Fathers" (written by an Episcopal priest to celebrate the 100th anniversary of the U.S. Declaration of Independence) and "O God, Beneath Thy Guiding Hand." The latter furthers the myth of the U.S. as a "Christian" nation as it speaks of God's guidance as "our exiled fathers crossed the sea" to bring "laws, freedom, truth, and faith in God" to the new land. Immediately after that song, Rev. J. McDowell Richards, a Presbyterian who served as president of Columbia Theological Seminary (a Presbyterian school), offered a prayer thanking God for the "heritage of devotion to Jesus Christ" by U.S. founders who "built a nation on justice and mercy."[13] He also thanked God for guiding the founders and having "overcome their enemies." Other songs suggested a less nationalistic vision by reminding the assembled congregation that "In Christ There is No East or West" and "Jesus Shall Reign Where'er the Sun."

One worship service during the NCC inaugural convention included the reading of a message from the U.S. president. Shortly before that, Methodist Bishop Ivan Lee Holt offered a "prayer for the nation." He prayed for the nation's leaders to follow God and for the nation to serve as a witness for God: "Endue with the spirit of wisdom those to whom in thy name we entrust the authority of government, that there may be justice and peace at home, and that through obedience to thy law we may show forth thy praise among the nations of the earth."[14]

President Harry Truman's message to the NCC meeting congratulated them on its creation and expressed hope that it would add to the impact churches have on the life of the nation. The NCC crafted an official response—voted on by delegates during the meeting—to send back to Truman, expressing prayers for him and his decisions. They added in their statement to Truman that they "express the fervent hope that the United States ... may act under God to secure with justice the enduring welfare of mankind."[15] After the meeting, Truman replied again, this time embracing the theme: "With true insight, your thoughtful body perceives that the United

---

[13] *Christian Faith in Action*, 55.
[14] *Christian Faith in Action*, 56.
[15] *Christian Faith in Action*, 148.

States, under God, is the world's last best hope for peace and for the welfare of the human race."[16] Truman's secretary of state also sent a message. Dean Acheson, son of an Episcopal bishop, praised the "historic importance" of the NCC's creation and talked about the "strategy of freedom" necessary to win the Korean War and prevent the Soviet Union from expanding its influence.[17]

Ambassador Francis Sayre (a U.S. representative to the United Nations, son-in-law to Woodrow Wilson, and a lay Episcopalian whose son would the next year become dean of the Washington National Cathedral), spoke to the NCC gathering, arguing "it is imperative that [the U.S.] stand as a Christian nation."[18] Sayre also demonstrated how Christian Nationalism ends up diluting or negating core Christian teachings, insisting that "it will not do to hold the principles taught by Christ applicable to individual men and women and not to nations."[19] But then he gave the "Christian nation" a pass from core principles taught by Christ: "The international problems of today are so amazingly complex, so tremendous in their scope, that one cannot expect Christianity overnight to yield a simple or rule-of-thumb answer in each case. Turning one's cheek, for instance, is not manifestly the sound solution for the problem of Korea."[20] The issue, he explained, is that "a Christian nation" must be careful in how it will "deal with an anti-Christian nation."[21] Apparently, a "Christian nation" doesn't actually have to act like Christ, especially when dealing with a non-Christian nation. But he nonetheless insisted the U.S. still gets to claim the Christian title.

"America has faced grave crises before. We remember Valley Forge, Gettysburg, Verdun, Pearl Harbor. Whatever may come, there is nothing to fear if only we have a stalwart faith in God and the courage to uphold Christian principles, even if necessary at the cost of life. 'Be strong in the Lord, and in the strength of his might,'" Sayre said,[22] adding a quote from Paul's writing about the "armor of God" in Ephesians 6.

---

[16] *Christian Faith in Action*, 149.
[17] *Christian Faith in Action*, 87.
[18] *Christian Faith in Action*, 121.
[19] *Christian Faith in Action*, 122.
[20] *Christian Faith in Action*, 125.
[21] *Christian Faith in Action*, 126.
[22] *Christian Faith in Action*, 128.

Several clergy who spoke during the meeting echoed the Christian Nationalistic themes of the messages from political figures. For instance, Rev. Hermann Morse, a Presbyterian minister who was elected as one of the first NCC vice presidents and who would shortly thereafter serve as moderator of the Presbyterian Church (U.S.A.), spoke about the mission "to make this a Christian nation."[23] He argued the NCC could play a critical role in this development: "We dare to believe that a Christian and a Protestant America can be the strongest force in the world against the new and the old paganisms that are contending for the mastery of the world."[24]

Rev. Henry Knox Sherrill, the NCC's first president and the presiding bishop of the Episcopal Church, similarly sounded the message about the U.S. as a supposed Christian nation.

"The Council marks a new and great determination that the American way will be increasingly the Christian way, for such is our heritage," he said in comments before his election as NCC president. "The Cleveland convention signifies a great first step. Together the churches can move forward to the goal: a Christian America in a Christian world."[25]

He repeated a version of the latter line later in his remarks after being elected president as he talked about what it means to have a nation "under God." Sherrill and the rest of the attendees wouldn't have to wait too long until they got to officially pledge allegiance to this nation "under God."

An Inspirational Sermon

The inaugural convention of the National Council of Churches wasn't the only push for declaring the nation to be "under God," though it does represent well the prevailing attitude of mainline Protestant leaders. The first National Prayer Breakfast in 1953 was held with the theme "Government Under God." And numerous other events were held conveying similar messages, along with sermons, proclamations, and pamphlets describing the nation in such terms.

For instance, in 1952, Sen. O.K. Armstrong, a Southern Baptist from Missouri, put in the *Congressional Record* various remarks from

---

[23] *Christian Faith in Action*, 95.
[24] *Christian Faith in Action*, 94.
[25] *Christian Faith in Action*, 11.

a recent gathering in Washington, D.C., of clergy from across the country. In introducing the remarks, Armstong noted the "theme of the pilgrimage was 'This Nation Under God.'"[26] And he noted that one part of the program was a meeting at National City Christian Church, the national church of the Disciples of Christ, that included remarks by U.S. Sens. Mike Monroney (an Episcopalian) of Oklahoma and Francis Case (a Methodist) of South Dakota, as well as the reading of statements from nine individuals running for president in that year's election (that would see Eisenhower move into the White House). Knowing they were sending messages to ministers, the candidates highlighted spiritual themes.

"The foundations of our nation were laid by men and women who believed in God, in his influence in human affairs," wrote Illinois Gov. Adlai Stevenson, who attended Unitarian and Presbyterian churches and became the Democratic presidential nominee that year. "America and its leaders believe in God; the rulers of Russia have turned their backs upon God and deny his very existence."[27]

Other candidates sent similar comments, with several emphasizing the theme of the nation being "under God." Like California Gov. Earl Warren, who the next year would become chief justice of the U.S. Supreme Court: "Our government is a government 'under God.' Our basic documents proclaim it. Our founding fathers made it a reality. Successive generations of Americans have tried to live a life under God."[28]

With the Cold War raging, the idea of marking the nation as "under God" continued to gain steam. U.S. Rep. Louis Rabaut, a Catholic from Michigan, introduced legislation in 1953 to put the phrase in the Pledge of Allegiance (although his initial proposal put a comma between "nation" and "under" that was later dropped). A Gallup poll that year found that 69% of Americans approved adding it, with just 21% opposed.[29] And Gallup found Protestants slightly more supportive of the proposal than Catholics, while younger

---

[26] *Congressional Record: Proceedings and Debates of the 82nd Congress, Second Session* 98 (1952): A2798.

[27] *Congressional Record*, 1952, A2798.

[28] *Congressional Record*, 1952, A2797.

[29] Lydia Saad, "Gallup Vault: Americans Favored Putting God in U.S. Pledge," Gallup, October 5, 2017, https://news.gallup.com/vault/220232/gallup-vault-americans-favored-putting-god-pledge.aspx.

Americans and those with college education were slightly less likely to back it than those who were older or with less education. Clearly, the time was ripe for such a change. But it would take a sermon to make it happen.

Rev. George Docherty of New York Avenue Presbyterian Church in Washington, D.C., preached to the 1952 pilgrimage that had included the session at National City Christian Church. In his remarks to the pastors during a session at his church, he drew from Lincoln's Gettysburg Address (the same line that inspired the first NCC meeting theme) and talked about the need to put "under God" in the Pledge. Docherty had grown up in Scotland chanting "God save the King," so he was surprised not to find a similar mix of faith and nationalism in the United States. He was encouraged by the feedback from the pastors but disappointed no one did anything about it.[30] Less than two years later, he prepared for a Sunday service knowing that Eisenhower would be sitting in the pew. Not just any pew. In "Lincoln's pew." Since the 16th president had worshiped there, the church had developed a tradition of getting presidents to show up for "Lincoln Sunday" in early February near Lincoln's birthday. So on February 7, 1954, Docherty dusted off his "under God" sermon to preach primarily to a powerful audience of one.

Lincoln "claims that it is 'under God' that this nation shall know a new birth of freedom," Docherty proclaimed. "And by implication, it is under God that 'government of the people, by the people, and for the people shall not perish from the earth.' For Lincoln, since God was in his heaven, all must ultimately be right for his country."[31]

Defining "the American way of life" as based on the Ten Commandments and "the words of Jesus of Nazareth, the living Word of God for the world," Docherty insisted Lincoln also saw this as what it meant to understand America. But the preacher lamented that such an understanding cannot be found in the Pledge:

> I came to a strange conclusion. There was something missing in this Pledge, and that which was missing was the characteristic and definitive factor in the American way of

---

[30] George M. Docherty, *I've Seen the Day* (Grand Rapids: William B. Eerdmans Publishing Co, 1984).

[31] *Congressional Record: Proceedings and Debates of the 83rd Congress, Second Session* 100 (1954), A1794

life. Indeed, apart from the mention of the phrase, the United States of America, this could be a pledge of any republic. In fact, I could hear little Muscovites repeat a similar pledge to their hammer-and-sickle flag in Moscow with equal solemnity, for Russia is also a republic that claims to have overthrown the tyranny of kingship.

The absence of "God" in the Pledge was particularly a problem, Docherty added, because he believed "we face today a theological war."[32] He insisted such a war went beyond the conflict between democracy and communism: "It is Armageddon, a battle of the gods. It is the view of man as it comes down to us from Judeo-Christian civilization in mortal combat against modern, secularized, godless humanity. ... To omit the words 'under God' in the Pledge of Allegiance is to omit the definitive character of the American way of life."

Having made his argument, Docherty continued in his sermon to argue why his proposal did not violate the separation of church and state. He insisted it was okay since it didn't pick a specific church. But after admitting the language would seem to exclude an atheist, he still defended the proposal with blatant Christian Nationalism:

> Philosophically speaking, an atheistic American is a contradiction in terms. ... They really are spiritual parasites. And I mean no term of abuse in this. I'm simply classifying them. A parasite is an organism that lives upon the life force of another organism without contributing to the life of the other. These excellent ethical seculars are living upon the accumulated spiritual capital of Judeo-Christian civilization, and at the same time, deny the God who revealed the divine principles upon which the ethics of this country grow. The dilemma of the secular is quite simple. He cannot deny the Christian revelation and logically live by the Christian ethic. And if he denies the Christian ethic, he falls short of the American ideal of life.

Docherty defined atheists as inherently un-American and even anti-American simply because of their theological beliefs. His call to add "under God" thus also was a push to undermine the meaning of "indivisible." But at least he said the quiet part out

---

[32] *Congressional Record*, 1954, A1795.

loud. Putting "under God" in the Pledge was intended to mark the U.S. as a "Christian" nation and to intermingle what it means to be an American and a Christian. And this call for codifying Christian Nationalism came from a pastor at a prominent Presbyterian church (his predecessor had been the influential Peter Marshall, a chaplain of the U.S. Senate and the subject of the book *A Man Called Peter*).

The sermon worked. Docherty's fellow Presbyterian, the president of the United States, quickly endorsed it. Then things took off. As historian Kevin Kruse wrote in *One Nation Under God*:

> The next morning, the offices of senators and representatives phoned the pastor to request copies of his sermon; it was soon reprinted in the *Congressional Record* and distributed widely. A Paramount Pictures recording of the event played in newsreel segments in theaters across the country for weeks afterward. The Hearst newspaper chain launched a major editorial campaign in favor of the change, while several radio commentators pressed the issue as well.[33]

(In contrast, we're happy when our sermons are still remembered the next week.) Soon, several Republican and Democratic members of Congress introduced bills, all hoping to get credit for the upcoming change in the Pledge. Eisenhower signed the change into law on Flag Day, June 14, 1954, as members of Congress celebrated on the steps of the Capitol with the new Pledge and the playing of "Onward, Christian Soldiers."[34] Barely four months had passed since Docherty's sermon. After six decades without "God," the Pledge got quickly baptized as the nation was being reborn with Christian Nationalistic flare.

Taking the Lord's Name

In 2002, as the nation debated President George W. Bush's desire to invade Iraq, the Christian community found itself divided. Many evangelicals backed the invasion, especially the Southern Baptist Convention which quickly emerged as the war's greatest religious cheerleader.[35] Meanwhile, many mainline Protestant leaders spoke

---

[33] Kevin M. Kruse, *One Nation Under God: How Corporate America Invented Christian America* (New York: Basic Books, 2015), 107.

[34] Kruse, *One Nation Under God*.

[35] Brian Kaylor and Bryan Fisher, "Onward Christian Soldiers: Southern Baptist Convention's Support for Operation Iraqi Freedom," *Journal of the Speech & Theatre Association of Missouri* 37 (2007): 61–77.

against the war, including Bush's own United Methodist Church. As this sparring unfolded, Rev. George Docherty took to the pulpit at Huntingdon Presbyterian Church in Pennsylvania. The pastor, who was then 91, had a long record of opposing war: as a pacifist in Great Britain during World War II, marching with Martin Luther King Jr. in Selma, and speaking early against the Vietnam War. But this sermon wasn't about Iraq. Instead, he was giving a repeat performance of the "under God" sermon he had given to Eisenhower over 48 years earlier.

The reason for the encore sermon was a recent decision by the U.S. Court of Appeals for the Ninth Circuit (which we referenced in chapter 3). In 2000, Michael Newdow filed a suit challenging the phrase "under God" in the Pledge as unconstitutional. He directed his suit toward the public school district where his daughter was enrolled and that daily recited the Pledge. As an atheist—whom Docherty had defined as inherently unAmerican and parasitic—Newdow argued the Pledge violated his right to teach his daughter religious beliefs. This is the same suit that eventually led to the resignation of the faith advisor for the Democratic National Committee in 2004 because she expressed support for Newdow's position. On June 26, 2002, the Ninth Circuit ruled 2-1 in Newdow's favor. About 150 members of the U.S. House of Representatives marched out to the Capitol steps to loudly recite the Pledge and sing "God Bless America." Democratic Sen. Robert Byrd of West Virginia, the only member of Congress who had actually been there in 1954 to vote for the inclusion of "under God" (and who had also served as an American Baptist Sunday School teacher), blasted the "stupid judges" who made the decision and promised to never vote to give them a higher office.[36]

Thirty-six senators cosponsored a bill expressing support for keeping "under God" in the Pledge. It quickly passed the Senate on a 99-0 vote, and then the House by 401-5. Bush signed the bill, though it didn't actually change anything. In between the Senate and House votes, Docherty returned to a Presbyterian pulpit to make the case for "under God" in the Pledge. War was on the horizon, but first Christian Nationalism needed saving.

---

[36] Carl Hulse, "Lawmakers Vow to Fight Judges' Ruling on the Pledge," *New York Times*, June 27, 2002, https://www.nytimes.com/2002/06/27/us/lawmakers-vow-to-fight-judges-ruling-on-the-pledge.html.

"My sermon itself is not important, but the significance of it is important: Is this a God-fearing nation or is it an atheistic one?" he said ahead of preaching it again in 2002.[37]

More than 400 people packed the sanctuary, a crowd usually seen there only on Christmas Eve or Easter. Despite the changes of the previous half-century, they gathered to reaffirm and celebrate the role of Presbyterians in putting "God" in the Pledge. And, of course, the congregation said the Pledge during the service while facing an American flag near the pulpit. Ultimately, neither Docherty's reunion sermon nor the congressional actions mattered. In 2004, the U.S. Supreme Court ruled against Newdow on technical grounds, claiming he didn't have standing. Docherty's phrase could stand. The U.S. would officially remain this nation under God.

Although a minority opinion, a handful of ministers argued for removing "under God." Thirty-two Christian and Jewish ministers (including the future DNC faith advisor) and the Unitarian Universalist Association submitted an amicus curiae brief to the Supreme Court urging such an action. Several mainline Protestant ministers joined the brief. They didn't use the term "Christian Nationalism," which wasn't in vogue, but the ministers did argue against confusing religious and nationalistic identities. They explained that the inclusion of "under God" in the Pledge meant that "the chosen form by which the nation requests a profession of loyalty also requests a profession of religious faith."[38] This therefore "put individual citizens in the position of being unable to affirm their loyalty to the nation unless they also affirm their belief in God." Such a dilemma, the ministers added, is even worse when placed on public school students:

> If a child cannot in conscience affirm the existence of a single God and God's authority over the nation, that child cannot affirm his loyalty to the nation in the legally prescribed form. The inevitable implication is that children who have doubts about God are of doubtful loyalty to the nation. ... Either government is asking school children to make a

---

[37] Mike Joseph, "Retired Pastor Takes Up Fight for 'Under God,'" *Centre Daily Times*, August 14, 2002, 11.

[38] *Elk Grove Unified School District v. Michael A Newdow*, https://supreme.findlaw.com/static/fi/images/efile/supreme/briefs/02-1624/02-1624.mer.ami.bailey.pdf.

sincere statement of belief in the one true God whom the nation is under, or it is asking children to take the name of the Lord in vain.

Preach it!

Chapter 6

IN GOD WE TRUST?

After Buffalo Bills player Damar Hamlin collapsed on the football field while suffering cardiac arrest in January 2023, Louisiana State Rep. Jack McFarland knew he needed to file new legislation. But the bill he quickly cosponsored had nothing to do with the New Orleans Saints or even athletics in general. Instead, he wanted to require every public school classroom in the Pelican State to post the national motto.

"That was a defining moment for a lot of people," McFarland explained about Hamlin's collapse. "The game just completely stopped and everybody put everything to the side."[1]

"I just think there are certain things in this country we can all get behind," he added. "Why would we not want to teach our children about the national motto?"

McFarland joined with fellow Republican—and fellow evangelical Southern Baptist—State Rep. Dodie Horton to make the effort to put the national motto in every classroom one of the very first bills of the 2023 legislative session. Several states already required posting the national motto in every public school—including Louisiana where lawmakers passed that requirement in 2018 and it was signed into law by the state's Democratic governor. But in 2023, there were calls to go a step further and make sure it

---

[1] Wesley Muller, "Louisiana Lawmakers Want 'In God We Trust' Signs in Every Classroom," *Louisiana Illuminator*, January 13, 2023, https://lailluminator.com/briefs/louisiana-lawmakers-want-in-god-we-trust-signs-in-every-classroom.

was visible not just in the hallways where students walked but from the desks in which they sat.

The year 2018 was when the Christian Nationalistic effort known as "Project Blitz" launched, even receiving an approving tweet the next year from President Donald Trump.[2] The effort's stated purpose is "to protect the free exercise of traditional Judeo-Christian religious values and beliefs in the public square,"[3] which it accomplishes by advancing model bills that state lawmakers can copy and paste to enshrine Christian Nationalistic ideas into law. Their legislation has included pushing the teaching of the Bible in public schools, giving healthcare workers and adoption and foster care agencies the right to discriminate while receiving government funds, and putting "In God We Trust" on license plates and in public schools. Due to the dogged reporting of researchers like Frederick Clarkson,[4] the Project Blitz effort eventually became so controversial they stopped using that name. But they are still pushing their legislative and policy goals.

Many states—including Arkansas, Florida, Kentucky, Louisiana, Mississippi, South Carolina, South Dakota, Tennessee, Utah, and Virginia—now mandate that public schools post the national motto, with most of the legislation passing since 2018. New bills continue to show up each year. Additionally, states like Ohio and Texas require the motto to be posted if someone donates the sign (so as not to use public funds). A few other states have passed bills encouraging, but not requiring, schools to post the motto. Such legislation has been sponsored by Republican and Democratic lawmakers, and signed by governors from both parties. The laws usually require its posting just one time per school in a "prominent" location. However, Mississippi requires it in every classroom, auditorium, and cafeteria (which seems like a strange way to address the state's last-in-the-nation status for K-12 education.) Unsatisfied with just one poster per school building in Louisiana, Horton and McFarland decided to require the phrase in every classroom.

---

[2] Donald Trump (@realDonaldTrump), January 28, 2019, https://twitter.com/realDonaldTrump/status/1089876055224184833.

[3] Congressional Prayer Caucus Foundation, https://cpcfoundation.com/first-freedom-coalition-project-blitz.

[4] Follow Clarkson's work on Project Blitz at https://www.blitzwatch.org.

"The signs are up usually near the office, but I've asked my grandkids if they've ever seen it and they said 'no,'" Horton explained. "But they will see these in their classrooms."[5]

Given where children devote their attention, the better strategy for achieving her goal would be mandating that Apple install it as the background on the next iPhone (we hope no politician writes a bill to implement our joke). But that demonstrates the absurdity of her quest. She claims to want the youth of Louisiana to see the motto because she believes it "sends an important message to our children as a sign of hope." But, of course, that's not what the national motto actually conveys. And when asked about church-state concerns with pushing a declaration about God in the classrooms, Horton insisted it's not a problem.

"I'm not asking you to accept my God or pushing religion on anyone," she said. "I just want children to see that there is a Creator. I don't see it as a controversial bill."

She also called it "one of the most non-controversial bills that you'll see my name attached to."[6] Which is quite an assertion considering the previous year she filed bills to name part of a highway after a firefighter who died on duty, increase how much money someone can make preparing foods at home under the cottage food law, and create a "Louisiana Wild Turkey Federation" specialty license plate (okay, so maybe that last one seems a bit … fowl).

Despite our skepticism, the legislation ultimately passed the Republican-led state House of Representatives with a whopping 98-4 vote and the Republican-led state Senate with a unanimous 37-0 vote. John Bel Edwards, the state's Democratic governor, then signed it, putting the new requirement into effect on August 1,

---

[5] Greg Hilburn, "Representative Dodie Horton Wants In God We Trust Displayed in Every Louisiana Classroom," *Lafayette Daily Advertiser*, January 19, 2023, https://www.theadvertiser.com/story/news/2023/01/19/louisiana-lawmaker-files-bill-to-put-god-in-every-school-classroom/69821507007.

[6] Brooke Thorington, "A Bill to Require 'In God We Trust' in Every Louisiana Classroom Among Legislation Filed for Upcoming Session," Louisiana Radio Network, January 16, 2023, https://louisianaradionetwork.com/2023/01/16/a-bill-to-require-in-god-we-trust-in-every-louisiana-classroom-among-legislation-filed-for-upcoming-session.

2023. It seems few things can bring two warring political parties together like posters of "In God We Trust." But while these bills often find bipartisan support, that doesn't mean they aren't considered controversial. Even many Christians speak out and testify against such legislation. For instance, Amanda Tyler, executive director of the Baptist Joint Committee for Religious Liberty, spoke against it in 2022 as her home state of Texas implemented its new law on the matter:

> I think this is an example of Christian Nationalism being put right into our public schools. And it's concerning because it is targeted at our most impressionable neighbors: children in public schools. ... Why this is so problematic is because it sends this message that to fully belong in our society and in our public schools, that one must have a certain religious perspective.[7]

But Horton and McFarland apparently aren't bothered by the notion of sending a problematic message to students. And both lawmakers justified their bill by noting the presence of the phrase "In God We Trust" on U.S. currency.

"Every religion identifies some type of god, whether in the Bible or Quran," McFarland—who apparently has never met a Buddhist—inaccurately argued. "I'm just asking them to believe in our national motto that's good enough to be printed on our currency. Why can it not be displayed in our classroom?"[8]

"It's our national motto; it's on our money," Horton said. "I really like the history behind it."[9]

The appeal to the phrase being on our currency is a common rhetorical tactic these days by those espousing Christian Nationalism—even when pushing things other than posting the phrase itself. For instance, as Ben Carson spoke during the 2016 Republican National Convention, he argued people should vote for Donald Trump as the candidate Carson believed best embodied our nation's religious character. He added, "This is a nation where our

---

[7] Laura Rice, "Why this Christian Leader Says Texas 'In God We Trust' Sign Debate is Symbolic of 'Christian Nationalism,'" *Texas Standard*, September 12, 2022, https://www.texasstandard.org/stories/texas-in-god-we-trust-sign-debate-symbolic-christian-nationalism-says-amanda-tyler.

[8] Muller, "Louisiana Lawmakers Want 'In God We Trust.'"

[9] Hilburn, "Representative Dodie Horton Wants In God We Trust."

Pledge of Allegiance says we are 'one nation under God.' This is a nation where every coin in our pocket and every bill in our wallet say 'In God We Trust.'"[10] When Trump wanted to argue during the 2018 National Prayer Breakfast that America follows God, he marshaled the same alleged evidence: "Our currency declares, 'In God We Trust.' And we place our hands on our hearts as we recite the Pledge of Allegiance and proclaim we are 'one nation under God.'"[11] And Fox News host Jeanine Pirro declared in 2022: "Look, this is a country founded on Judeo-Christian, ok? This is in my courtroom and most courtrooms in this country. They say 'In God We Trust.' It's even on our money."[12]

Despite Pirro's suggestion, the appearance of the phrase on our money and in our courtrooms doesn't date to our founding. And while Horton said she really likes the history behind it, we wonder if she's familiar with the actual record. It's a story about war. And mainline Protestants.

An Uncivil Move

The preamble to the Constitution of the Confederate States of America framed the new breakaway country as a Christian nation. It noted the people of the Confederacy were "invoking the favor and guidance of Almighty God" to "ordain and establish this Constitution for the Confederate States of America."[13] It marked a substantive shift away from what some people called the "godless" Constitution of the U.S., which referred to religion in its original version only by prohibiting religious tests for public office. So as the Civil War started, some Christians in the North worried that God might favor

[10] Ed Kilgore, "This Is Why Ben Carson Was Talking about Lucifer at the RNC," *New York Magazine*, July 20, 2016, https://nymag.com/intelligencer/2016/07/why-ben-carson-was-talking-about-lucifer-at-rnc.html.

[11] "Remarks by President Trump at the 66th National Prayer Breakfast," February 8, 2018, https://trumpwhitehouse.archives.gov/briefings-statements/remarks-president-trump-66th-annual-national-prayer-breakfast.

[12] Michael Luciano, "Jeanine Pirro Claims the U.S. was 'Founded on Judeo-Christian ethics' by Alluding to Law Enacted in 1955," *Mediaite*, July 7, 2022, https://www.mediaite.com/tv/jeanine-pirro-claims-the-u-s-was-founded-on-judeo-christian-ethics-by-alluding-to-a-law-enacted-in-1955.

[13] "Constitution of the Confederate States; March 11, 1861, The Avalon Project, https://avalon.law.yale.edu/19th_century/csa_csa.asp.

the Confederates. This line of thinking suggested that they needed to do something to invoke—and perhaps even demand—God's blessing on the side of the Union.

In the early months of the war, Rev. Mark Watkinson sent a letter dated November 13, 1861, to the U.S. secretary of the treasury with one such solution: put God on Mammon. And who was Watkinson? The pastor of First Particular Baptist Church (now known as Prospect Hill Baptist Church) in Prospect Park, Pennsylvania. The congregation is affiliated with the American Baptist Churches USA (who back then were known as Northern Baptists).

"One fact touching our currency has hitherto been seriously overlooked. I mean the recognition of the Almighty God in some form on our coins," Watkinson wrote to the Treasury secretary. "You are probably a Christian. What if our Republic were not shattered beyond reconstruction? Would not the antiquaries of succeeding centuries rightly reason from our past that we were a heathen nation?"[14]

Thus, Watkinson suggested a redesign that would include "God, Liberty, Law" stamped on the money. The minister even suggested it could help with the war effort.

"This would make a beautiful coin, to which no possible citizen could object," he added in his letter. "This would relieve us from the ignominy of heathenism. This would place us openly under the Divine protection we have personally claimed. From my heart I have felt our national shame in disowning God as not the least of our present national disasters."

Treasury Secretary Salmon Chase agreed with the general argument. A lifelong Episcopalian, Chase was raised in his teen years by his uncle, who was an Episcopal bishop. Chase wrote a November 20, 1861, memo to James Pollock, the director of the U.S. Mint, to find a suitable way to invoke God on the coins of the Union.

"No nation can be strong except in the strength of God, or safe except in his defense. The trust of our people in God should be declared on our national coins," Chase wrote. "You will cause a device to be prepared without unnecessary delay with a motto expressing in the fewest and tersest words possible this national recognition."[15]

---

[14] "History of 'In God We Trust," U.S. Department of the Treasury, https://web.archive.org/web/20160417102334/https://www.treasury. gov/about/education/Pages/in-god-we-trust.aspx.

[15] "History of 'In God We Trust," U.S. Department of the Treasury.

Pollock was of a similar mind as Watkinson the Baptist pastor and Chase the lay Episcopalian. The former governor of Pennsylvania, Pollock was a lifelong Presbyterian who served as an elder in his local church and while leading the Mint was vice president of the American Sunday School Union that promoted the creation of Sunday School programs in churches. Drawing from the last stanza of "The Star-Spangled Banner," Pollock suggested the motto "In God Is Our Trust." That song, of course, had also been penned during wartime as Francis Scott Key, an Episcopalian, composed it while witnessing the shelling of Fort McHenry during the War of 1812.

"We claim to be a Christian nation," Pollock wrote in an 1863 report suggesting a conversion of the coin design to add his God motto. "Why should we not vindicate our character, by honoring the God of nations, in the exercise of our political sovereignty as a nation? Our national coinage should do this. Its legends and devices should declare our trust in God; in him who is the 'King of kings and Lord of lords.'"[16]

Like Watkinson and Chase, Pollock also tied the need to put God on the coins to the hope of winning the Civil War.

"The time for the introduction of this or a similar motto is propitious and appropriate," he argued. "'Tis an hour of national peril and danger, an hour when man's strength is weakness, when our strength and our nation's strength and salvation must be in the God of battles and of nations. Let us reverently acknowledge his sovereignty, and let our coinage declare our trust in God."

Chase liked the idea, but he crossed out the "is our" in Pollock's motto and wrote "we." The next year, 1864, Congress approved the new design, and "In God We Trust" showed up on two-cent coins as the war with Confederate forces continued. The slogan didn't initially appear on all money, just on coins. And not everyone approved. A *New York Times* editorial in 1865 criticized "the enactment of this new form of national worship" as "improper."[17] The piece added, "Let us

---

[16] *Report of the Secretary of the Treasury, on the State of Finances for the Year Ending June 30, 1863* (Washington: Government Printing Office, 1863), 190.

[17] "The New Legend on Our Coins," *New York Times*, December 18, 1865, https://www.nytimes.com/1865/12/18/archives/the-new-legend-on-our-coins.html.

try to carry our religion—such as it is—in our hearts, and not in our pockets." Others joked about trusting in God but demanding cash.

President Theodore Roosevelt removed the phrase from coins in 1907 as part of an attempt to beautify the coins, but public outrage led to the slogan returning the next year. An Episcopal layman in Pennsylvania spearheaded the campaign to return God to the coins, and pastors across the country preached against Roosevelt's redesign.[18] Prominent critics of Roosevelt's move included banker and Episcopalian J.P. Morgan, Democratic U.S. Rep. Morris Sheppard (a Methodist who later became known as "the father of Prohibition" for authoring the Eighteenth Amendment), and the vestry of the Episcopal Church in Richmond, Virginia (where Patrick Henry gave his famous "give me liberty or give me death" speech). Additionally, denominational groups passed resolutions calling on the return of God on U.S. coins, including the Episcopal Diocese of New York and the Presbyterian Brotherhood of America.

After first showing up during the Civil War (and surviving Roosevelt), the phrase "In God We Trust" would soon soar to national significance well beyond coins jingling in pockets. And another war would provide the inspiration.

Spreading the Word

The years just after World War II ushered in a golden age for Christian Nationalism in the United States. After the creation of the National Day of Prayer in 1952, the launch of the National Prayer Breakfast in 1953, and the addition of "under God" to the Pledge of Allegiance in 1954, the revival spread to feature "In God We Trust."

On April 8, 1954, President Dwight Eisenhower became the first president to participate in a ceremony unveiling a new postage stamp. And what stamp rose to such significance? The first regular U.S. stamp with a religious message. The new 8-cent Liberty stamp featured a drawing of the Statue of Liberty from the waist up with the word "Liberty" just below her. But arching over the top of her head was the phrase "In God We Trust." Postmaster General Arthur Summerfield, a Presbyterian, opened the official governmental ceremony by inviting Rev. Roy Ross to give an invocation. Ross,

---

[18] Willard B. Gatewood, "Theodore Roosevelt and the Coinage Controversy," *American Quarterly* 18, no. 1 (1966): 35–51, https://doi.org/10.2307/2711109.

a Disciples of Christ minister, was at the time the leader of the National Council of Churches. Ross prayed that Americans would "always prove ourselves a people mindful of thy favor and glad to do thy will."[19]

"Oh God, imbue with the spirit of wisdom those to whom in thy name we entrust the authority of government," Ross added before blessing the stamp as an evangelistic platform. "Grant that this new instrument which we dedicate this day may present an effective message of faith and freedom throughout the whole wide world."

Summerfield pointed to the unusual attendance of governmental officials and religious leaders as proof of the importance of the new stamp that "symbolizes the rededication of our faith in the spiritual foundations upon which our government and our nation rest."[20] He added, "It is fitting this stamp will be used extensively for foreign mail because we want men of good will everywhere to know that America will always remain a God-fearing, God-loving nation where freedom and equality for all are living and imperishable concepts."

Helping to emphasize the goal of this stamp signaling a global message amid the Cold War, Secretary of State John Foster Dulles then spoke. The son of a Presbyterian minister, Dulles was active in his church and the Federal Council of Churches (later the National Council of Churches). During the stamp ceremony, he specifically highlighted the importance of the stamp saying "In God We Trust" since "this linking together of political liberty and morality is fundamental to our nation."[21]

"This stamp is a small object, but its significance is great," Dulles added. "Today, when despotism holds one-third of the peoples of the world in its grip, it is important that we remind ourselves of the great truths upon which our freedom rests."

Catholic Cardinal Francis Spellman of New York echoed a similar message as he referred to "In God We Trust" as "our national motto" (which we're getting to but hadn't officially happened yet). He added that he prayed this stamp would result in "inspiring shackled peoples everywhere now living in terror of godless tyrants fearlessly

---

[19] *Congressional Record: Proceedings and Debates of the 83rd Congress, Second Session* 100 (1954): 4868.

[20] *Congressional Record*, 4868.

[21] *Congressional Record*, 4868.

unfalteringly to follow the one road to freedom and salvation through trust in God."[22]

Eisenhower used his presidential bully pulpit to bring greater attention to the new stamp and the religious message it sent about the United States. NBC carried the event live on TV, and Vice President Richard Nixon hosted a lunch for the hundreds of people who attended the ceremony. During Eisenhower's brief remarks, he highlighted how a governmental stamp could be an evangelizing tool:

> Throughout its history, America's greatness has been based upon a spiritual quality, which seems to me is best symbolized by the stamp that will be issued today. ...[The stamp] gives to every single citizen of the United States, as I see it, the chance to send a message to another. Regardless of any eloquence of the words that may be inside the letter, on the outside he places a message: "Here is the land of liberty and the land that lives in respect for the Almighty's mercy to us."[23]

After Summerfield gave Eisenhower the first set of the new stamps, Rabbi Norman Salit closed the ceremony in prayer.

Later that day, Sen. Frank Carlson of Kansas, an American Baptist layman serving as chair of the National Prayer Breakfast, took to the Senate floor to announce the "impressive service" that had occurred to unveil the stamp and he put the transcript of the entire event in the *Congressional Record*.[24] Sen. Charles Potter, a Methodist from Michigan, also spoke to the Senate about the stamp that day. He had authored legislation leading to the stamp. He praised "the most impressive" ceremony and the message that will now be "sent to people throughout the world on a little postage stamp" that "we as, as Americans, believe in spiritual values" and "we are a great nation because of our belief and trust in God."[25]

All of this might seem like a bit much for a postage stamp. But the effort to enlist "In God We Trust" in a crusade against the "godless" Soviet Union was just starting. The next year, 1955, U.S. Rep. Charles Bennett of Florida introduced a bill to require "In God We Trust"

---

[22] *Congressional Record*, 4868–4869.
[23] *Congressional Record*, 4869.
[24] *Congressional Record*, 4867.
[25] *Congressional Record*, 4868.

be printed on all paper money in addition to on coins. A member
of a Disciples of Christ congregation, he had built a reputation as a
voice for morality and faith in the House. His fellow Disciple, Sen.
William Fulbright of Arkansas, carried the bill through the Senate
where it received unanimous support. Eisenhower signed the bill
in July of that year, though the first redesigned new bills didn't roll
off the presses until 1957.

While the Treasury Department worked to add God to our
greenbacks, Congress made an even bigger move. Just days after
Eisenhower had signed the currency bill, Bennett started working on
a new bill: one to make "In God We Trust" the official national motto.
Bennett told his congressional colleagues that choosing that over
the unofficial older motto, "E Pluribus Unum," should be supported
since it "would keep us constantly reminded of the spiritual and
moral values upon which our country was founded and upon which
it depends for survival."[26] It took some pushing, but he got the bill
through the House and Senate with little opposition. Eisenhower
signed it into law on July 30, 1956.

"In little more than two years' time, 'In God We Trust' had surged
to public notice, first taking a place of prominence on stamps and
currency, and then edging its way past 'E Pluribus Unum' to become
the nation's first official motto," historian Kevin Kruse wrote in *One
Nation Under God*. "The concept of unity from diversity could not
compete with that of unity from divinity." [27]

While many evangelicals today point to "In God We Trust" on our
money and in our motto to justify their vision of a Christian nation,
mainline Protestants first perfected that argument for decades
before and after Eisenhower put his signature on the motto bill. For
instance, during a prayer to start the House session on September
11, 1963, Chaplain Frederick Brown Harris, a Methodist, declared
that the lawmakers "bow at this altar of prayer because in our hearts
we know that the destiny of this nation is inseparably bound up with
loyalty to its national heritage. That heritage is rooted in thee."[28] He
added in his prayer:

[26] Kevin Kruse, *One Nation Under God: How Corporate America
Invented Christian America* (New York: Basic, 2015), 122.
[27] Kruse, *One Nation Under God*, 124.
[28] *Congressional Record: Proceedings and Debates of the 88th
Congress, First Session* 109 (1964): 16764

Stab our spirits broad awake to a compelling realization
that the greatest spiritual task that confronts the lawmaking
bodies of the land is in interpreting for these times in which
we are called to serve the awesome meaning of the motto,
inscribed on the money which crosses our counters of trade,
"In God We Trust," and in applying that stupendous trust
to our national and international life. So make our hearts
strong whatever the future may hold. We ask in the spirit
of Christ. Amen.

Other congressional prayers over the years similarly invoked "In
God We Trust" as a binding creed.

But this story shouldn't be separated from war. Christian
Nationalism both fuels war and finds power during war. From the
War of 1812 to the Civil War to the Cold War, efforts to conscript God
helped lay the foundation for Christian Nationalism today. And it's
not just "In God We Trust." One of us (Brian) once studied the uses
of the phrase "God Bless America" in the paper of public record, the
New York Times.[29] Finding nearly 1,800 incidents over 123 years,
the study showed how the phrase was overwhelmingly used in
patriotic/nationalistic ways instead of to communicate a religious
message. The primary driver of the phrase's popularity was war.
Graphing usages of the phrase by year showed that World War II
and September 11, 2001, dominated the landscape, with smaller
peaks during Vietnam and World War I. Soldiers and military leaders
were quoted using the phrase more than clergy—while celebrities,
politicians, and athletes more commonly appeared as the speakers.
Although Irving Berlin originally wrote the song as an anthem to
promote peace, it quickly morphed into an anthem that cheers as
the nation fights war after war. As the study concludes:

The phrase "God Bless America" becomes a call to action
during difficult times of crisis in order to unite the people
and reestablish the nationalistic pride and confidence. The
ideologically powerful phrase is not merely decorative but
instead serves as an important unifying action to rally the
nation in support of military policies and operations. ...

[29] Brian T. Kaylor, "'God Bless America' Serves to Rally Americans to
War," *Newspaper Research Journal* 34, no. 2 (2013): 93-105, https://doi.
org/10.1177/073953291303400.

Thus, "God Bless America" is less of a prayer or statement of religious fervor than it is a sign of complete devotion to the nation. Irving Berlin's peace song has turned into an American battle cry.[30]

The same is true with "In God We Trust," "under God," and other Christian Nationalistic symbols. They are less about God than about nationalism. And they've consistently served to drum up support for wars and rumors of wars. Trying to invoke divine blessing to win wars, Christian Nationalism sanctifies violence. The more truthful motto might be "In War We Trust."

An Enduring Legacy

When James Pollock, the head of the U.S. Mint during the Civil War, was a congressman in the 1840s, he supported the efforts of Samuel Morse in developing the telegraph. As Morse sent the first message, Pollock was in the room where it happened. From the U.S. Capitol, Morse sent a message to Baltimore: "What hath God wrought?" The phrase came from Numbers 23:23 in one of the messages of Balaam, the diviner with the talking donkey. Had Pollock been in the Capitol 177 years later, he might have seen several people carrying signs declaring "In God We Trust" as they stormed the Capitol on January 6, 2021. And on the infamous gallows built just outside the Capitol as people chanted "Hang Mike Pence," people wrote "Hang them for treason," "God Bless the USA," and "In God We Trust."[31]

Yet, even after that, some mainline Protestants continue to celebrate their role in helping establish this motto. Like Prospect Hill Baptist Church in Prospect Park, Pennsylvania, the church where Rev. Mark Watkinson served in 1861 as he started the push to put God on our money. With events being held outdoors during the COVID-19 pandemic, there was a sign of nostalgia for Christian Nationalism even as progressive agendas were being advanced. For instance, on Martin Luther King, Jr. Day in 2022, people stood outside the church and read King's "I Have a Dream" speech as part

---

[30] Kaylor, "'God Bless America,'"103.

[31] *Christian Nationalism and the January 6, 2021 Insurrection*, https://static1.squarespace.com/static/5cfea0017239e10001cd9639/t/6203f007e07275503964ab4d/1644425230442/Christian_Nationalism_and_the_Jan6_Insurrection-2-9-22.pdf.

of a community emphasis on combating racism. Above the speakers, an old sign hung on the exterior wall of the building: "Historic site. Origin of In God We Trust."[32] In smaller text beneath an image of two coins, the sign notes that "from this church in 1861 the suggestion was made that recognition to the Almighty God be placed on the coins of our country."

On a smaller scale, the website of First Presbyterian Church in Sunbury, Pennsylvania, brags on its history page that Pollock worshiped at the church early in his career before he later "originated" the effort to put "the motto, 'In God We Trust,' on the United States coins that went into the collection plates."[33] Aside from the fact that Chase, not Watkinson or Pollock, actually came up with the phrase "In God We Trust," the sign and website show how the efforts to create a significant Christian Nationalistic symbol are celebrated even today at mainline Protestant congregations. Far from a reckoning, the phrase is still lifted up.

But while these churches were ministering during COVID-19 and celebrating Epiphany, others also heralded "In God We Trust" as they participated in the Capitol insurrection. Once mustered up during the Civil War and Cold War, "In God We Trust" has worked for decades to bolster a Christian Nationalistic worldview among some Americans with its presence on numerous official documents and governmental buildings. Preaching from courtrooms, schools, currency, and presidential remarks, the motto adopted in wars today continues to disciple Americans to view their nation and faith in particular ways.

The phrase has survived multiple legal challenges to maintain its official status, but this has not always been a victory for Christianity. For instance, a 1970 federal appellate decision on a case questioning the phrase on currency found it didn't violate church-state separation because the phrase was just "of patriotic or ceremonial character" without "any religious significance" and "no theological or ritualistic impact."[34] And a 2005 appellate ruling rejected a challenge to

---

[32] See a photo from Paul K. Johnson on Facebook, January 17, 2022, https://www.facebook.com/photo?fbid=10159736908439708&set=p cb.10159736922639708.

[33] "First Presbyterian History," Sunbury First Presbyterian Church, http://sunburypresbyterianchurch.org/history.html.

[34] *Aronow v. United States* (1970).

government buildings posting the motto because the phrase had "a legitimate secular purpose."[35] Far from keeping God in society, by adopting "In God We Trust" our government managed to kick religion out of "God."

That's a key problem that ultimately emerges. In the quest to place "In God We Trust" in various public spaces, those pushing for it will argue it's a generic, unifying patriotic statement. The attempts to declare that the phrase "In God We Trust" is a religiously neutral statement is offensive. But it is precisely by defining it as secular that courts have backed use of the phrase on coins and public buildings. It's blasphemous to use that phrase as some broad, inclusive, unifying, generic American statement. Who is this "god" that the state is telling us to trust? To believe in God is by definition not religiously neutral. To conflate being American with being Christian is to attempt to water down—and even attack—the basic teachings of Christianity. But that's what Christian Nationalism does.

The phrase chosen during the Civil War to invoke God's blessings on the Union during the bloody fight against the Confederacy found itself in the crowd along with waving Confederate flags during an attempt to overturn an election. The insurrectionists, like religious and political leaders during the Cold War, held up as their motto a phrase that claimed God was on their side instead of a motto about the many people of the nation coming together as one. What hath God's people wrought?

---

[35] *Lambeth v. Board of Commr's of Davidson County* (2005).

Section III

HOW MAINLINE PROTESTANTS
BROUGHT STATE TO CHURCH

Chapter 7

SEEKING A BLESSING

Tear gas filled Lafayette Square on June 1, 2020. Showing little consideration for the First Amendment right to freely assemble, police and troops belonging to the National Guard cleared peaceful protesters from the public space immediately north of the White House. Shortly after the crowd dispersed, President Donald Trump and officials from his administration—including Attorney General William Barr and Chairman of the Joint Chiefs of Staff Mark Milley (in uniform)—paraded across the park so that Trump could stage a now infamous photo op holding up a Bible in front of St. John's Episcopal Church.

The sequence of events leading to this ominous moment began in late May 2020 when the park filled with people protesting the murder of George Floyd at the hands of Minneapolis police officers, broader issues of police brutality, and our society's continued struggles with racism. While largely peaceful, a minority of the protesters engaged in more provocative acts that captured Trump's attention. On May 29, some of the protesters threw objects at police, crossed barricades, and pulled down security fencing near the White House complex. As the Secret Service worked to control the volatile situation, the White House went on lockdown. The president and his family were relocated to a protective bunker. Two days later, protesters set fire to the Ashburton House, a historic home across the street from the park. The house is now owned by and connected to St. John's, which uses it for a variety of parish functions. The damage to the building proved relatively minimal.

"The protests that began peacefully grew to something more, and eventually a fire was lit in the nursery, in the basement of Ashburton House," explained Rev. Robert Fisher, the church's rector. "Protesters easily could have done a lot worse to our buildings, but they chose not to do that."[1]

Apparently, Trump didn't get Fisher's message.

"The church was badly hurt," he stated in an interview before sharing a post on Twitter falsely claiming that it "was firebombed by terrorists."[2]

Motivated by perceptions of weakness related to the bunker episode and with the arson as a pretext, Trump used St. John's as a photo opportunity to project strength. After people had been tear-gassed—including priests on the lawn of the church—Trump stood in front of the church and held up a Bible in a way that seemed to symbolically conflate imposed civil "law and order" with a book associated with the revelation of God's law. Protests and condemnations from many Christians, especially Episcopal leaders, quickly followed.

"[The Bible] almost looked like a prop," Bishop Mariann Budde of the Episcopal Diocese of Washington, in whose jurisdiction St. John's resides, told NPR. "That is the most sacred text of the Judeo-Christian tradition. It speaks messages of love of God, love of neighbor. I was outraged that he felt that he had the license to do that, and that he would abuse our sacred symbols and our sacred space in that way."[3]

Episcopal Presiding Bishop Michael Curry stated, "The president of the United States stood in front of St. John's Episcopal Church, lifted up a Bible, and had pictures of himself taken. In so doing, he used a

[1] Sophia Barnes, "Historic Church Near White House Damaged Amid Unrest; Leaders Pray for Healing," NBC 4 Washington, June 1, 2020, https://www.nbcwashington.com/news/local/historic-church-near-white-house-damaged-amid-unrest-leaders-pray-for-healing.

[2] Michael Shear and Katie Rogers, "Trump and Aides Try to Change the Narrative of the White House Protests," *New York Times*, September 1, 2020, https://www.nytimes.com/2020/06/03/us/politics/trump-protests.html.

[3] Tom Gjelten, "Peaceful Protesters Tear-Gassed to Clear Way for Trump Church Photo-Op," NPR, June 1, 2020, https://www.npr.org/2020/06/01/867532070/trumps-unannounced-church-visit-angers-church-officials.

church building and the Holy Bible for partisan political purposes. This was done in a time of deep hurt and pain in our country, and his action did nothing to help us or to heal us."[4]

What that outrage ignores is the history of St. John's, a congregation whose geographical proximity to the White House has created a complicated mix of identities revealed in the congregation's nickname as "the Church of the Presidents." The congregation's own website explains that "beginning with James Madison, until the present, every person who has held the office of President of the United States has attended a service at St. John's." The site adds that "pew 54 is the President's Pew, and is reserved for the president's use when in attendance at the church."[5] That designation of a reserved pew occurred due to the financial largess of former President John Tyler. He bought a pew subscription, permanently setting aside space at St. John's for the use of future presidents.[6] Since the mid-twentieth century, most presidents have worshiped at the church on the morning of their respective inaugurations, giving St. John's a prominent role in a service that imbues a day of national and political significance with sacred meaning as well.

Before controversially strolling across the cleared Lafayette Square and posing with the Bible, Donald Trump had previously visited St. John's on multiple occasions, including the day of his inauguration. For that service, the church turns the pulpit over to the choice of the new president. That means they didn't offer a prophetic warning as Trump took office but instead facilitated a sermon by Rev. Robert Jeffress, a Southern Baptist pastor known for controversial comments attacking Muslims, Mormons, and Catholics (and who said during the 2016 election he wanted Trump over Jesus: "I don't want some meek and mild leader or somebody who's going to turn

---

[4] Adam Raymond, "Trump Denounced for Using the Bible As a Prop," *New York Magazine*, June 2, 2020, https://nymag.com/intelligencer/2020/06/trump-bible-photo-op-has-religious-leaders-outraged.html.

[5] "History," St. John's Church, https://stjohns-dc.org/welcome-to-saint-johns-church/history.

[6] Erin Vanderhoof, "A Brief History of St. John's Episcopal Church, Site of Trump's Tear Gas Procession," *Vanity Fair*, June 2, 2020, https://www.vanityfair.com/style/2020/06/a-brief-history-of-st-johns-episcopal-church-trump-tear-gas.

the other cheek. I've said I want the meanest, toughest SOB I can find to protect this nation"[7]).

As distasteful as many found Trump's biblical stunt, the logic of a president seeing St. John's as a backdrop for sending a message and bolstering their support is not hard to grasp. It's a church that willingly plays an outsized and public role in the spiritual (and political) lives of U.S. presidents as it participates in presidential pageantry and affords presidents special status (including a reserved pew). Such treatment toward the commander-in-chief is difficult to square with the admonitions in the Book of James against offering the rich and powerful a privileged seat (2:2-4). It also conflicts with the church's own witness. Responding to Trump's stunt, the congregation displayed a banner in support of the Black Lives Matter movement.[8] Like many other mainline churches, St. John's emphasizes the relationship between faith and social engagement on issues like climate change and the plight of refugees.

Physically located across the park from the White House and on a street renamed for the Black Lives Matter movement, St. John's exists at a major tension point between church and state. Despite its social justice activism that seeks to alter the status quo, the congregation offers a unique form of legitimacy to the powers that be. It's difficult to simultaneously be Christ's Church and the Church of the Presidents. It's hard to serve in the king's court and also speak as the prophet.

In the Capital and of the Capital

While unusual, St. John's is not the only church—and not even the only Episcopal church—in Washington, D.C., that must wrestle with this conundrum. Like the "Church of the Presidents," the

[7] Michael Martin, "Pastor Robert Jeffress Explains His Support for Trump," NPR, October 16, 2016, https://www.npr.org/2016/10/16/498171498/pastor-robert-jeffress-explains-his-support-for-trump. Jeffress later even invited Trump into the pulpit at First Baptist Church in Dallas during a Sunday service six days before Christmas in 2021; see: Brian Kaylor and Beau Underwood, "Make Worship Great Again," *A Public Witness*, December 21, 2021, https://publicwitness.wordandway.org/p/make-worship-great-again.

[8] Melissa Howell, "St. John's Church Declares Support for Black Lives Matter Movement," WTOP News, June 10, 2020, https://wtop.com/dc/2020/06/st-johns-church-speaks-out-in-support-of-the-black-lives-matter-movement.

Washington National Cathedral's name bears witness to the inherent tension of existing as a Christian community in the nation's capital city.

The spiritual cornerstone of any church is Jesus Christ (Matt. 21:42). Still, someone has to lay a building's physical cornerstone. With thousands of people gathered for the spectacle in 1907, President Theodore Roosevelt addressed the crowd and observed the beginning of the cathedral's construction. Making clear the connections to the desired status of the cathedral, to which Congress had given a charter, workers used the same mallet to tap in the cornerstone as had been used on the cornerstone of the U.S. Capitol. Even with the building becoming operational, it took until 1990 for that construction to be completed. President George H.W. Bush was invited to help to mark the achievement. With presidents bookending the construction, the church demonstrated a key part of its identity and audience. Bush, an Episcopalian himself, clearly articulated Christian Nationalist sentiments in his speech:

> Here we have built our church—not just a church, a house of prayer for a nation built on the rock of religious faith, a nation we celebrate as "one nation under God," a nation whose founding president, George Washington, said: "No people can be bound to acknowledge and adore the invisible hand which conducts the affairs of men more than the people of the United States."[9]

Presidents and other political leaders are a regular presence at the cathedral. Like services at St. John's held at the start of inaugural festivities, prayer services the day after the inauguration are a common occurrence at the cathedral. And the sanctuary often hosts funerals when presidents and other prominent public figures pass away. Woodrow Wilson is even buried in the building's crypt.

Beyond these ceremonial functions, the country's presidents and political figures step into the cathedral's ornate pulpit for more substantive reasons as well. Three days after the terrorist attacks of September 11, it hosted a national prayer service that became

---

[9] George H.W. Bush, "Remarks at the Washington National Cathedral Dedication Ceremony," September 29, 1990, https://www.presidency. ucsb.edu/documents/remarks-the-washington-national-cathedral-dedication-ceremony.

a spiritual rally for marching into war. To the military, political, and religious leaders gathered, President George W. Bush declared from the pulpit that God would bless the nation's cause: "They have attacked America because we are freedom's home and defender, and the commitment of our fathers is now the calling of our time. On this National Day of Prayer and Remembrance, we ask Almighty God to watch over our nation and grant us patience and resolve in all that is to come."[10]

The other main preacher for the service joined the president in promising divine assistance in winning the coming war. Evangelist Billy Graham proclaimed, "We're facing a new kind of enemy. We're involved in a new kind of warfare. And we need the help of the Spirit of God. The Bible's words are our hope: 'God is our refuge and strength; an ever-present help in trouble.'" Graham added, "We also know that God is going to give wisdom and courage and strength to the president and those around him. And this is going to be a day that we will remember as a day of victory."[11]

Presidents—like everyone else—certainly deserve funerals that reflect their religious beliefs. And nations and their leaders should find ways to express their collective emotions, especially in moments of extreme grief and anger. The concern raised here is about the negative effects that follow when we too easily mix the sacred and the secular. Hindsight might be 20/20, but history has demonstrated the foreign policy and military failures that followed 9/11. Blindsided by an attack, the U.S. rushed into Afghanistan with only the vaguest of objectives that were never realized despite two decades of fighting, trillions of dollars spent, and civilian deaths that numbered in the tens of thousands. Even worse, America invaded Iraq under false pretenses, incurring even greater costs and damaging both international norms and the nation's reputation on the world stage. But this isn't just the wisdom of hindsight. There were Christian voices casting doubt on the wisdom of such zealousness.

"Bush said the war on terror 'will not end until every terrorist group of global reach has been found, stopped, and defeated.' Such an ambitious goal fails to pass the test of just war theory," argued

---

[10] "National Prayer Service," C-SPAN, September 14, 2001, https://www.c-span.org/video/?166031-1/national-prayer-service.
[11] "National Prayer Service," C-SPAN.

Robert Parham of the Baptist Center for Ethics in a September 2001 editorial. "The promise to rid the world of terrorism reflects the dangerous ideology of purity. It bumps against the line of holy war in which crusaders believe the world may be purified from evil."[12]

"Nonviolence and what it means to be a disciple of Christ are constitutive of one another," theologian and Duke University professor Stanley Hauerwas said to explain his opposition at the time to the Afghanistan mission. "So many people are on a kind of God-and-country bandwagon right now. That's very sad, from my point of view."[13]

Rather than serving as a similar voice of caution encouraging greater humility and discernment, the Washington National Cathedral hosted a prayer service that stoked the passions for war and blessed the impending military actions as a holy crusade. Yet, just years later a different message would be heard in its sanctuary. Thousands packed into its pews in March 2007 to observe the fourth anniversary of the Iraq War. Instead of using religious rhetoric to bolster the war's cause, the purpose of this occasion was the exact opposite: a large-scale protest of America's war involvements.

"This war, from a Christian point of view, is morally wrong— and was from the beginning," proclaimed Jim Wallis, the founder of Sojourners who now leads the Georgetown University Center on Faith and Justice. He also labeled it "an offense against God."[14]

"Mr. Bush, my Christian brother," Raphael Warnock, the senior pastor of Ebenezer Baptist Church in Atlanta who would later become a U.S. senator from Georgia, said, "we need a surge in the nonviolent army of the Lord. We need a surge in conscience and a surge in activism and a surge in truth-telling."[15]

---

[12] Robert Parham, "Was It a Word of Prophecy in 2001 that Afghan War Would Be Unsuccessful?," *Good Faith Media*, December 8, 2009, https://goodfaithmedia.org/was-it-a-word-of-prophecy-in-2001-that-afghan-war-would-be-unsuccessful-cms-15294.

[13] "Just War: Christian Ethicists: Afghan War Is Just," *Christianity Today*, March 11, 2002, https://www.christianitytoday.com/ct/2002/march11/19.23.html.

[14] Sarah Karush, "Christians Gather in Washington, D.C. for Protest Against Iraq War," *Seattle Times*, March 17, 2007, https://www.seattletimes.com/nation-world/christians-gather-in-washington-dc-for-protest-against-iraq-war.

[15] Karush, "Christians Gather in Washington, D.C."

A similar tension can be seen in the cathedral's treatment of Trump. They sparked controversy by participating in his inauguration activities in 2017, with the National Cathedral's Choir of Men, Boys, and Girls singing during the inaugural ceremony at the Capitol and the cathedral hosting a prayer service with Trump the next day.[16] While this progressive congregation hosted Trump in its sanctuary with Budde and the cathedral's dean, Randolph Marshall Hollerith, participating in a service ripe with patriotic hymns and uniformed military personnel, thousands of Americans protested in the streets of Washington, D.C., as part of the "Women's March" opposing Trump's rhetoric and policies. Hollerith would join Budde and Curry on numerous occasions in criticizing comments and actions by Trump, but only after first blessing him while others offered a prophetic warning about the character of the new leader.

These areas of dissonance exemplify the tension inherent in the cathedral's identity. Consider the self-description given under the "Who We Are" section of its own website: "Grounded in the reconciling love of Jesus Christ, Washington National Cathedral is a house of prayer for all people, conceived by our founders to serve as a great church for national purposes."[17] Such a statement seems unaware that contradictions might arise between what the "reconciling love of Jesus Christ" requires of "a great church" and the "national purposes" of a country led by fallible, self-interested human beings. This assumption of an easy connection between American and Christian identities is exactly the kind of fertile soil in which Christian Nationalism has grown.

The attempt to be both a house to worship Jesus and a house for all Americans simply isn't tenable. Richard Benjamin Crosby noted the "confusion of identity" in his book analyzing the cathedral and its history (though he sees it as part of the civil religious tradition instead of an exemplar of Christian Nationalism). He wrote:

> It is no wonder that in its attempt to administer the American Civil Religion, Washington National Cathedral

---

[16] Sarah Pulliam Bailey, "Some Upset over National Cathedral's Decision to Participate in Trump's Inauguration," *Washington Post*, January 13, 2017, https://www.washingtonpost.com/news/acts-of-faith/wp/2017/01/13/washington-national-cathedrals-decision-to-participate-in-trumps-inauguration-is-creating-tension.

[17] "Mission & Vision," Washington National Cathedral, https://cathedral.org/about/mission-vision.

often seems like a charioteer holding the reins of wrangling horses. Its effort to pilot the horses, or at least to keep them civil to one another, is admirable but tragic in a way. The cathedral is both religious and political, sectarian and nonsectarian, local and national, private and public. For over a century, it has tried to reconcile those priorities, to rein in the horses into a kind of harmony.[18]

Perhaps it's an impossible mission.

In reality, there are bound to be conflicts between the transcendent demands of the Christian gospel and the specific agenda of a country at a particular moment in history. The inherent risk in the cathedral's dual goals is struggling to navigate the tradeoffs. It's the challenge faced by any pastor when the mayor wants to speak or a civic group wants to hold an event in the church's space, but the profile of the National Cathedral immensely magnifies the conundrum. The cathedral brands itself as "A House of Prayer for All People." Seeking to be a prominent, neutral gathering place in Washington, D.C., for elite events is what creates confused moments where sacred space advances military triumphalism—replete with the singing of the "Battle Hymn of the Republic"—and later hosts hundreds of Christians who plan a mass arrest protesting war.

Moreover, the cathedral does not really intend to invite "all people" and all messages into its doors. Just like St. John's, the Washington National Cathedral hosts a worshiping community and enjoys an organizational life independent of its interaction with public leaders. In a number of ways, the cathedral has marshaled its resources in support of efforts to reduce gun violence and address racism in American society. For example, in 2017 it removed stained glass windows featuring Confederate generals and commissioned an artist to design replacements emphasizing racial justice that were installed in 2023. Presumably, the cathedral would not provide space for the president to speak to an NRA prayer service or invite a prayer meeting of White supremacists. Yet, the cathedral has sent the message that the decades-long "war on terror" was both a righteous Christian cause and an offense against God. Both of those

---

[18] Richard Benjamin Crosby, *American Kairos: Washington National Cathedral and the New Civil Religion* (Baltimore: Johns Hopkins University Press, 2023), 143.

things simply cannot be true. In seeking to serve national purposes, the cathedral faces the constant threat of compromising its integrity as a great church.

From the Good Book to the God Box

Shifting our attention away from the problem of presidents, pews, and pulpits, let's spend some time looking at how the Bible has been a tool for conflating mainline Christian witness with the work of the government. Here we don't mean the words of Scripture, but the actual book itself.

Imagine this scenario: It's 2020 and President Donald Trump hosts a group of evangelical Christians in the White House Rose Garden for a public event. The conservative faith leaders are there to celebrate a new Bible translation, and they want to present the president with the first copy. To much fanfare, they hand a Bible to Trump, and he praises the gift because he believes the teachings of Scripture support his policy agenda. The reaction from mainline and more progressive Christians would have been swift and understandable. The denouncements of state endorsement of religion and Christian Nationalism would have been loud, with severe admonishments leveled at Trump and the religious elites around him for their perceived exclusivity and insensitivities.

Something like this actually happened, but Trump was not the occupant of the White House. Back in 1952, representatives from the National Council of Churches had an event with President Harry Truman. The purpose was to celebrate the release of the Revised Standard Version of the Bible. The president would receive the very first copy that was printed. In remarks given in the Rose Garden on the afternoon of September 26, Truman expressed gratitude for the gift. But he went even further, telling those gathered that the teachings of the Bible were key to achieving his foreign policy aims:

> If people understood the contents of this book from cover to cover, and we could get a complete understanding of it behind the Iron Curtain, there would be but one thing in this world: peace for all mankind. Maybe we can accomplish that some time. I hope you gentlemen will keep working at it. I have made an effort on that subject for seven years,

to get the moral forces of the world in opposition to the unmoral forces.[19]

Those remarks are a textbook example of Christian Nationalism, even if that label for such an ideology was not then in vogue. Christian and American identities are perceived as mutually reinforcing.

While abstractly promoting peace, Truman presumed the kind of peace testified to in the Bible as being desired by God is the same peace that serves the interest of a particular nation. There's no awareness that, as Christians historically have understood it, the former is much broader than the latter. Moreover, there's an easy equation here of one's nation's actions as moral and others' as "unmoral," with the assumption that Christianity informs and blesses the efforts of the righteous ruler of the nation. Yet, it was Truman who ordered atomic bombs dropped on Japan, which resulted in tens of thousands of civilian deaths. In this moment, there was no acknowledgment of the morally ambiguous choices that he was forced to confront as president, nor how such actions contrast with the biblical teachings about loving one's enemies.

Rather than serving as a critical voice that acknowledges the world's inherent flaws or how all human creatures and creations— including governments and their leaders—fall short of the glory of God, Christianity is constructed here as providing moral legitimacy to all of Truman's record. And the Christian leaders sought, in turn, to bestow legitimacy upon their new translation as if the real moral authority needed for endorsement was the U.S. president. By handing him a Bible, the delegation from the National Council of Churches fostered the idea the United States and its president were divine instruments used for God's intended purpose. There's no daylight between the priorities of the country and the mission of the Church.

Fast forward to October 12, 1958. Again, the path of a president intersected with the work of the NCC. This time the setting was New York City. Dwight Eisenhower was present to lay the cornerstone for the Interchurch Center, a massive building that would become home to a variety of denominational, ecumenical, and interfaith

---

[19] Harry Truman, "Remarks to Representatives of the National Council of Churches," September 26, 1952, https://www.presidency.ucsb.edu/documents/remarks-representatives-the-national-council-churches.

organizations (including the NCC until 2013). Colloquially, the structure has become known as the "God Box" (which isn't meant as an architectural compliment).

Alongside various church leaders, Eisenhower addressed a crowd celebrating the occasion. His comments mostly steered clear of Christian Nationalistic ideas, but his mere presence is what the ministers presumably wanted as they sought to christen their new building as an important American landmark. Eisenhower emphasized the importance of religious liberty in relation to civic life. Still, he quoted the New Testament and referenced "our faith" in a way that reveals the dominant Christian ethos of the time.

"That cornerstone symbolizes a prime support of our faith—'The Truth' that sets men free. The freedom of a citizen and the freedom of a religious believer are more than intimately related; they are mutually dependent," Eisenhower claimed.[20]

In his defense of religious liberty, he included a strong denouncement of a synagogue bombing that had happened earlier that morning in Atlanta, Georgia:

> We are politically free people because each of us is free to express his individual faith. As Washington said in 1793, so we can say today: "We have abundant reason to rejoice that in this land the light of truth and reason has triumphed over the power of bigotry and superstition, and that every person may here worship God according to the dictates of his own heart." ... Can you imagine the outrage that would have been expressed by our first president today, had he read in the news dispatches of the bombing of a synagogue?

Yet, these relatively inclusive remarks found ways to exclude certain Americans who did not adhere to the religious norms of society. Namely, they defined national identity as including only those who rooted their personal beliefs in religious convictions. As Eisenhower stated near the conclusion of his speech, "Our first president spoke gratefully of religious liberty, but he spoke also of the moral requirements which religion places on the shoulders of

---

[20] Dwight Eisenhower, "Remarks at the Cornerstone-Laying Ceremony for the Interchurch Center, New York City," October 12, 1958, https://www.presidency.ucsb.edu/documents/remarks-the-cornerstone-laying-ceremony-for-the-interchurch-center-new-york-city.

each citizen, singly and together. Washington believed that national morality could not be maintained without a firm foundation of religious principle."

Even at the opening of a building designed to foster understanding and collaboration across denominations and faiths, the subtle message expressed by the president of the United States was that to count as a good American, one needs to be religious. That invites the more important question: Why was a president asked to lay the cornerstone at the Interchurch Center in the first place? And why did mainline and other Christian leaders want to give the first copy of the RSV Bible to the president? What does each side get from these public interactions?

Proximity and Power

Political leaders have long understood the value of religious support for enhancing their rule. Whether imperial cults that claimed emperors to be divine, or kings and queens who claimed a divine right to their thrones, history is filled with examples of state authorities using religion to sanction and strengthen their power. It's not a stretch to assume that in accepting the very first edition of the RSV Bible in the Oval Office or laying the cornerstone at the Interchurch Center or speaking from the pulpit at the National Cathedral or raising a Bible in front of St. John's that Harry Truman, Dwight Eisenhower, George W. Bush, and Donald Trump all sought this kind of blessing. They recognized that appearing with faith leaders in religious places alongside sacred symbols made their actions and administration look moral, perhaps even holy, to those watching and listening. But why do Christian leaders in the U.S.— especially mainline Protestants—cooperate? Why are they so willing to let themselves be used in this way?

Calling Christian Nationalism by another name, American religious historian Mark Toulouse wrote at length about the idea of "priestly faith," which "confuses the nation with the church" by "understand[ing] important national values to be normative for the church."[21] He explained, "The priests of this faith assume authority and know all the answers because they are the experts

---

[21] Mark Toulouse, *God in Public: Four Ways American Christianity and Public Life Relate* (Louisville: Westminster, 2006), 78.

in the American cultural tradition."[22] While more conservative or fundamentalist Christians are often perceived as acting in this way, Toulouse rightly noted that "religious liberals have been known to practice it on occasion."[23] Indeed, there was a season when mainline Protestantism assumed it shaped and reflected the dominant American ethos. They created what historian David Sehat called "a moral establishment that connected religion and the state" and "claimed that God's will should determine the parameters of American freedom, which opened the door to serious encroachment on American liberty."[24] Other scholars have similarly noted this majoritarian societal role of mainline Protestantism.

"The terms *mainline* and *civic* have long been seen as nearly synonymous," wrote sociologist Nancy Ammerman. "Churches in the historic Protestant 'mainstream' have drawn on both their theological heritage and their position at the center of American culture to make unique contributions to the well-being of our society."[25]

This perceived agreement between church and society made it easy to practice the kind of soft, supposedly benevolent form of Christian Nationalism highlighted in this chapter. Yet, the last several decades have revealed the fracturing of that relationship and the challenges from evangelical and other conservative Christians claiming to better represent American and Christian identities.[26] The mainline has been pushed to the sideline in a way that reveals the dangers of seeking to function as priests of the American faith.

Among the many unanticipated aspects of Trump's rise was the strong support he received from evangelical voters. A thrice-married man with a history of lewd remarks, questionable business practices, and other character defects was not the most obvious political hero for socially conservative voters to rally around. Despite those

[22] Toulouse, *God in Public*, 79.
[23] Toulouse, *God in Public*, 79–80.
[24] David Sehat, *The Myth of American Religious Freedom,* updated edition (Oxford: Oxford University Press, 2015), 5–6.
[25] Nancy Ammerman, "Connecting Mainline Protestant Churches with Public Life," in *The Quiet Hand of God: Faith-Based Activism and the Public Role of Mainline Protestantism*, ed. Robert Wuthnow and John H. Evans (Berkley: University of California Press, 2002), 129.
[26] David Hollinger, *Christianity's American Fate: How Religion Became More Conservative and Society More Secular* (Princeton: Princeton University Press, 2022).

shortcomings, a large number of prominent faith leaders embraced Trump's candidacy. He received the absolution their endorsements provided to their followers and the broader electorate, while they received access and sway over his administration's agenda. Like with any other interest group, the transactional nature of politics was on clear display.

But influence can be illusionary, even as access is seductive. Historian John Fea labeled Trump's most vocal and prominent religious supporters as "court evangelicals" because the functions they took on resembled those of clergy who served kings in bygone eras.[27] Their ceremonial roles aided Trump's political fortunes but regularly made the religious leaders look morally compromised or hypocritical as they became overtly partisan figures who had to defend the sordid details of his personal life, frequent offensive remarks, and policies that contradicted core tenets of Jesus's teachings.

Like any human beings, Christian laypeople and clergy can become intoxicated by politics. An invitation to the White House or a photo with the president confers legitimacy and increases prominence. Such privileges come with a cost. Staying in the good graces of power usually requires shifting one's loyalties and sacrificing one's witness.

Mainline and progressive Christians correctly castigate evangelical or conservative leaders who render to Caesar what belongs to Jesus. Yet, they miss both the subtle and obvious ways, historically and in the present, they also participate in being priests of American culture rather than proclaimers of the gospel. The state and its leaders will always welcome what bolsters their image and secures their position. In exchange for transforming the secular into the appearance of something sacred, religious leaders believe they receive increased access to power and wider audiences for their messages. In reality, they end up preaching a Christian Nationalism that undermines their cause. Mainline Protestants in the United States are far from immune from this disease that threatens Christ's Church. In fact, in many ways they were the superspreaders who passed the virus on to Trump's court evangelicals.

---

[27] John Fea, *Believe Me: The Evangelical Road to Donald Trump* (Grand Rapids: Eerdmans, 2018).

Chapter 8

WORSHIPING AMERICA

On July 4, 1976—the 200th anniversary of the Declaration of Independence—churches across the country devoted their Sunday worship services to Bicentennial commemorations. Months of celebrations of the nation's birth culminated on that Fourth of July. With essentially every area of society joining the party, many congregations dedicated their worship services to recognizing the national holiday. From singing patriotic hymns to inviting politicians as guest speakers to talk about the country, there was little distinction between church and state. Like at Independence Boulevard Christian Church, a Disciples of Christ congregation in Kansas City, Missouri. Their guest preacher for the Bicentennial Sunday was U.S. Rep. Jerry Litton, a Presbyterian who was a rising star in the Democratic Party and in the middle of a primary battle for a U.S. Senate seat.

"It is particularly important that those in government give some kind of reassurance to the people that God has not forsaken our government and that government has not forsaken God," Litton declared.[1]

Noting political upheavals and concerns about the future of the nation, he insisted that despite it all there were still signs of the Christian nature of the country. He gave some examples, all of church and state intermingling that mainline Protestants helped establish. And throughout his remarks, he worked in humorous quips and

---

[1] "Jerry Sutton Sermon at K.C. Church 1976," Grand River Historical Society Museum's Facebook page, https://www.facebook.com/watch/?v=533777191424397.

classic midwestern farmer tales that teach morals about faith, hard work, and living a good life.

"You might be pleased or perhaps surprised to know that every session of the House and the Senate is opened with a prayer. And many talk about the government taking prayer out of school and taking God out of government, and in spite of all of that we open every session of the House and the Senate with a prayer. Some suggest that it's the only occasion during the entire course of the day when the Congress knows what it's doing," he said, with the last line provoking some laughter.

Litton also told the congregation about the prayer room near the chambers in the Capitol. Noting all the tourists who would visit Washington, D.C., that year but not go to the prayer room on the tours, he added, "The one thing that they will not see most probably is the one thing they perhaps ought to see." He called the prayer room "a chapel that is distinct because only 535 people are permitted to worship in it." That room was created in 1953, right around the time of several other efforts to put God in government and American public life. Rep. Brooks Hays (a Southern Baptist from Arkansas) introduced a House resolution calling for its creation while U.S. Sen. Mike Monroney (an Episcopalian from Oklahoma) introduced the companion resolution in the Senate. During the floor discussion about the proposal, multiple lawmakers quoted the Bible to justify creating a congressional chapel, including Psalm 127 about needing the Lord to build the house and Matthew 6 where Jesus urged his followers to pray (secretly in a closet). Following the passage of the resolutions, House Speaker Joseph Martin Jr. (a Catholic from Massachusetts) designated a room to be the chapel, which opened in 1955.

To plan its new design, Martin appointed a committee of Hays, Rep. Karl LeCompte (a Methodist from Iowa), and Rep. Katharine St. George (an Episcopalian from New York). An advisory committee included House Chaplain Bernard Braskamp (a Presbyterian) and Senate Chaplain Frederick Brown Harris (a Methodist), along with a Catholic and a Jewish representative since both chaplains were mainline Protestants. The room includes a stained-glass window depicting George Washington kneeling in prayer with the words of Psalm 16:1 around him: "Preserve me, O God, for in thee do I put my trust." Above him is a phrase from Abraham Lincoln's Gettysburg Address: "This Nation Under God." On the altar below that sits a Christian Bible. The website of current House Chaplain Margaret Kibben (a Presbyterian), links the room today to other efforts to mark the nation as God's:

> Just as prayer was offered at the constitutional convention and is still offered today at the beginning of each session of Congress; just as the ministry of chaplains of all faiths serve our men and women in the military; just as our coinage, the Pledge of Allegiance, and our postage stamps witness our faith in Divine Providence, so too does the prayer room give the men and women who have the gravest decisions to make for America and the world an opportunity to be alone with God.[2]

That's the room Litton gushed about to the Disciples on the Bicentennial. He added about the room: "It might surprise many in this country to know that the chapel is often used. And during those times of difficult votes, many a member of the House and the Senate would go to the chapel to seek help."

But despite these signs of involving God in government that Litton found encouraging, he also lamented that in the nation overall "somehow we've lost faith in our God and our country." He argued that the Bicentennial and the Fourth of July celebrations were the perfect time to recapture "the thrill that used to be there when the flag passed and the National Anthem was sung. And maybe we can recover also that same kind of deep faith in God that used to be so terribly important to the basic structures of this country. And we so badly need it." For Litton, the Bicentennial of the founding of the nation became the perfect time for a national religious revival, where faith in God and faith in the nation went hand-in-hand.

The church service featuring Litton was hardly an anomaly on that Bicentennial Sunday. Congregations across the country waved their flags—sometimes literally—as they celebrated America. Baptizing the birth of the nation as a divine act, these services preached a Christian Nationalistic gospel. For instance, those at the

---

[2] "Congressional Prayer Room," Office of the Chaplain, United States House of Representatives, https://chaplain.house.gov/religion/prayer_room.html.

1973 general convention of the Episcopal Church passed a resolution encouraging the denomination and churches to start preparing for Bicentennial celebrations three years later. The Episcopal Church also published a book of worship liturgies, prayers, and suggested songs for congregations to highlight the Bicentennial during the Fourth of July service and other occasions during the year. The book's title? *This Nation Under God: A Book of Aids to Worship in the Bicentennial Year 1976.* So pulpits across the country celebrated a mix of God and country similar to what Rep. Litton offered the Disciples gathered in Kansas City.

One month after his Bicentennial sermon, Litton won the Democratic primary for the U.S. Senate seat opening up because the incumbent was retiring. Litton had defeated another U.S. representative (and son of the retiring senator) and a former governor. However, his plane crashed that night on the way to his victory party, killing the 39-year-old politician, his wife, their two children, and two others. The state Democratic leaders chose the runner-up, former Gov. Warren Hearnes as the replacement candidate, but he lost that November to Missouri's Republican Attorney General John Danforth. An Episcopal priest, Danforth had been the preacher for an ecumenical bicentennial prayer service in Ferguson, Missouri, on July 4 as the kickoff to the Independence Day festivities in the St. Louis suburb that Sunday morning.

Decades later, Danforth became a fierce critic of the mixing of religion and politics by conservative evangelicals as a result of "the takeover of the Republican Party by the Christian Right."[3] As he in 2005 blamed the Christian Right for "the collapse of bipartisan collegiality" in Congress, he wrote:

> Many conservative Christians approach politics with a certainty that they know God's truth, and that they can advance the kingdom of God through governmental action. So they have developed a political agenda that they believe advances God's kingdom, one that includes efforts to 'put God back' into the public square and to pass a constitutional amendment intended to protect marriage from the

---

[3] John C. Danforth, *Faith and Politics: How the 'Moral Values' Debate Divides America and How to Move Forward Together* (New York: Penguin Group, 2006), 7.

perceived threat of homosexuality. ... To assert that I am on God's side and you are not, that I know God's will and you do not, and that I will use the power of government to advance my understanding of God's kingdom is certain to produce hostility.[4]

More recently, Danforth the retired politician preached during a Methodist church service and warned about making politics an idol, insisting, "There can only be one ultimate concern." He added, "For Christians, it's the kingdom of God. When we make anything else ultimate, we violate the second commandment, we commit idolatry. In Old Testament times, people made idols of gold and silver. Today, we make idols of ideology and politics. Surely politics is important, but we should not make it our ultimate concern. It isn't religion."[5]

Danforth has rightly critiqued the ways conservative evangelicals have polarized politics and pushed sectarian faith expression in government in divisive ways. But as he contrasts politics today with his time in office, he generally fails to assess how his fellow mainline Protestants first helped create such Christian Nationalism—albeit a more collegial and bipartisan form. Danforth has confessed that he shouldn't have spoken in conservative churches during campaigns since he went "not really to worship but to appeal for votes."[6] Noting that candidates of both parties do this—just at different churches—he added, "The candidate is using the church for political purposes, and the church is conforming itself to this world." Just as partisan politics is often welcomed into sanctuaries during elections, Christian Nationalism has often been embedded in worship services like on the Bicentennial Sunday. If we listen carefully, we'll hear Christian Nationalism in the sermons, prayers, liturgies, and songs not only in evangelical and Pentecostal congregations but also in many mainline Protestant churches.

---

[4] John C. Danforth, "Onward, Moderate Christian Soldiers," *New York Times*, June 17, 2005, https://www.nytimes.com/2005/06/17/opinion/onward-moderate-christian-soldiers.html.

[5] Brian Kaylor, "In Sermon, Former U.S. Sen. John Danforth Decries 'Holy War' Politics," *A Public Witness*, October 24, 2022, https://publicwitness.wordandway.org/p/in-sermon-former-us-sen-john-danforth

[6] Danforth, *Faith and Politics*, 214.

Off-Key

Fanny Crosby was the most prolific hymn writer of the nineteenth century and perhaps of any time—despite being blind from infancy. She wrote more than 8,000 hymns, many of which still show up in numerous church services every week, like "Blessed Assurance," "Jesus Is Tenderly Calling You Home," "Pass Me Not, O Gentle Savior," "Rescue the Perishing, Care for the Dying," and "To God Be the Glory." Her words appear in most hymnals across denominational lines. But the Methodist Episcopal layperson also wrote more than 1,000 secular poems as well as political and patriotic hymns.

During the Civil War, the New Yorker penned several songs that pushed the Union's cause. She wrote pro-Union lyrics to the popular "Dixie" tune to encourage soldiers to rally against the traitors. In "There's a Sound Among the Forest Trees," another song written to encourage people to join the Union forces, Crosby invoked "the Pilgrim fathers" and suggested heavenly support for the Union's cause: "There's an angel form above us gently twining a wreath for the conqueror's brow." Similarly, in "Song to Jeff Davis," she dared the Confederate leader to show himself with his soldiers when "we'll blow thy ranks to atoms." She added why she knew the "traitor band" would lose: "Our stars and stripes are weaving, and Heav'n will speed our cause."

Even when not cheering for soldiers, Crosby's tunes sometimes got patriotic. Like her song "Our Country" first published in 1868. The first stanza describes the beauty of the nation's mountains, rivers, lakes, woodlands, and eagles. It opens with the declaration, "Our country, unrivaled in beauty and splendor that cannot be told."[7] The next verses switch to history, painting the U.S.'s founding as based on God. Crosby called America "the birthplace of freedom" and spent more than half a verse praising George Washington:

Mount Vernon, where Washington slumbers,
The soul of thy freedom for years,
A willow droops tenderly o'er him,
Go hallow his grave with thy tears;
Go hallow his grave with thy tears.

---

[7] https://hymnary.org/text/our_country_unrivaled_in_beauty.

The last verse combines beauty and history to declare the nation characterized "with ardent devotion" to God. Crosby added:

In him be the strength of our nation,
His laws and its counsel its guide.
Our banner, that time-honored banner,
That floats o'er the ocean's bright foam
God keep them unsullied forever,
Our standard, our union, our home;
Our standard, our union, our home.

Unlike her war songs, this one showed up in several hymnals, including one published by a denomination that eventually became part of the United Methodist Church, a hymnal published by Disciples of Christ musician William E. Hackleman, and several hymnals edited by Disciples of Christ minister and songwriter Christopher Columbus Cline. One of Cline's hymnals with the song was *Popular Hymns, Number 2* published in 1901 by the Christian Publishing Company in St. Louis, Missouri (the forerunner to today's Chalice Press, which published the book you're now reading). In the latter hymnal, "Our Country" is the first song in the section "Special Songs for Special Occasions." The first six songs get the subheading of "National," with later songs for occasions like "temperance" and "miscellaneous" (the temperance songs are the most unusual with selections like "He's a Drunkard To-night" and "Come Home, Father"). The other nationalistic songs for churches to sing in worship services or Sunday School classes are "America" (or "My Country, 'Tis of Thee"), "The Star-Spangled Banner" (which wouldn't actually be the official National Anthem for another three decades but was written by an Episcopalian), two songs praying for peace (but that aren't actually nationalistic in tone), and a lyric called "Keller's American Hymn" to be sung to the tune of one of the peace hymns. Other hymnals call that song, written and composed during the Civil War, "Speed Our Republic."

1. *Speed our Republic, O Father on high!*
   Lead us in pathways of justice and right;
   Rulers as well as the ruled, one and all,
   Girdle with virtue—the armor of might!
   Hail! Three times hail to our country and flag!

2.   Foremost in battle, for freedom to stand,
     We rush to arms when aroused by its call;
     Still as of yore, when George Washington led,
     Thunders our war-cry, we conquer or fall!
     Hail! Three times hail to our country and flag!

3.   Rise up, proud eagle, rise up to the clouds,
     Spread thy broad wings o'er this fair western world!
     Fling from thy beak our dear banner of old!
     Show that it still is for freedom unfurled!
     Hail! Three times hail to our country and flag![8]

The song appeared in several other hymnals early in the twentieth century, including ones published by Methodist publishing house Abingdon Press and the American Baptist publishing house Judson Press. But both Crosby's "Country" and Keller's hymn pale in popularity among songbooks then and now when it comes to patriotic tunes.

Consider the popularity of "My Country, 'Tis of Thee," written by American Baptist minister and journalist Samuel Francis Smith to the tune of "God Save the King." First performed during an 1831 Fourth of July celebration at a church in Boston, it has since been published in more than 1,900 hymnals.[9] The National Anthem hasn't been quite as popular, but has appeared in more than 400 hymnals.[10] Other patriotic hymns that didn't make it in the 1901 songbook from the Christian Publishing Company have also proved popular. "America the Beautiful" is in about 500 hymnals.[11] "God of Our Fathers," written by an Episcopal priest and released by the Episcopal Church as the chosen hymn to celebrate the centennial of the U.S. Constitution, has been published in more than 400 hymnals.[12] And Julia Ward Howe's "Battle Hymn of the Republic," written for Union soldiers at the suggestion of a Unitarian minister, has shown up in more than 500 hymnals.[13]

[8] https://hymnary.org/text/speed_our_republic_o_father_on_high.
[9] https://hymnary.org/text/my_country_tis_of_thee_sweet_land.
[10] https://hymnary.org/text/o_say_can_you_see_by_the_dawns_early_lig.
[11] https://hymnary.org/text/o_beautiful_for_spacious_skies.
[12] https://hymnary.org/text/god_of_our_fathers_whose_almighty_hand.
[13] https://hymnary.org/text/mine_eyes_have_seen_the_glory.

These nationalistic songs appear in pretty much every mainline Protestant denomination's hymnals today. The 1995 *Chalice Hymnal* includes "America the Beautiful," "God of Our Fathers," "Battle Hymn of the Republic," and "My Country, 'Tis of Thee." Both the current United Methodist Church hymnal from 1989 and the most recent Presbyterian Church (U.S.A.) hymnal from 2013 include those four songs. The latest hymnal of the Episcopal Church from 1982 doesn't include "Battle Hymn of the Republic" but does have the other three songs. Additionally, the Episcopal hymnal includes the National Anthem, printed with the first and fourth verses (the latter being the one with the line, "And this be our motto—'In God is our trust'"). It also includes the hymn "God Bless Our Native Land." The words are by a German poet in the early nineteenth century, but this version sets it to the tune of "My Country, 'Tis of Thee," thus helping make the land in question the United States:

> God bless our native land;
> firm may she ever stand
> thro' storm and night!
> When the wild tempests rave,
> Ruler of wind and wave,
> Do thou our country save,
> By thy great might![14]

Interestingly, the hymnal includes only the first two verses that are nationalistic but not the third stanza which expands the vision:

> And may the nations see
> That men should brothers be,
> And form one family!
> God save us all!

That song—again with just the first two verses—also appears in the latest hymnal of the Evangelical Lutheran Church in America from 2006. Nearby sit "America the Beautiful" and "Battle Hymn of the Republic." And "O Canada!" made it in. Christian Nationalism can cross borders.

The inclusion of such songs in our hymnals isn't merely innocent patriotism. By placing an official imprimatur on these nationalistic hymns in a book used for holy worship, denominational publishers

---

[14] https://hymnary.org/text/god_bless_our_native_land_firm_may_she.

and church leaders helped stress the "and" in God and country. The inclusion of such songs discipled generations of churchgoers that America was uniquely blessed by God and that allegiance to the U.S. was as much of the Christian calling as the other doctrines taught in the hymnal, like the importance of celebrating Advent, trusting in Jesus, and believing in the empty tomb. The songs teach Christian Nationalism in a way that is more effective for many people—through music. Let's consider some of the problematic lines from a medley not unlike what one might hear on the Sunday closest to the Fourth of July:

> *America! America! God shed his grace on thee,*
> *and crown thy good with brotherhood*
> *from sea to shining sea.*
> *My native country, thee,*
> *land of the noble free,*
> *thy name I love;*
> *I love thy rocks and rills,*
> *thy woods and templed hills;*
> *my heart with rapture thrills*
> *like that above.*
> *Thy love divine hath led us in the past;*
> *in this free land with thee our lot is cast;*
> *be thou our ruler, guardian, guide, and stay,*
> *thy word our law, thy paths our chosen way.*
> *As he died to make us holy, let us die that all be free!*
> *While God is marching on.*
> *O beautiful for heroes proved*
> *in liberating strife,*
> *who more than self their country loved,*
> *and mercy more than life!*
> *America! America! May God thy gold refine,*
> *till all success be nobleness,*
> *and every gain divine.*

The songs glorify America and at times even sing praises to the nation and the nation's natural beauty instead of praising the Creator. The pilgrims and other "fathers" of the past are referenced, with the implication that they intended to create this nation as a Christian land. Perhaps most problematically, some of the songs baptize the death of soldiers for the nation as a Christian sacrifice. Although noble, such deaths are not salvific nor on par with the death of Christ. Conflating the two types of sacrifices is common in Christian Nationalistic rhetoric where to die for one's country is inherently to die for God—even if it involves non-Christian soldiers or if it means killing Christians on the other side of the border.

The publishing of such hymns—and the continued inclusion of them—is not something that happens by chance. Official denominational hymnals are typically only produced every couple of decades or longer. A large committee spends years considering which songs should stay, leave, or be added. It's a process that considers not only popularity and styles but also theology. For instance, when the Presbyterian Church (U.S.A.) released its 2013 hymnal, it sparked controversy over the exclusion of "In Christ Alone," a popular hymn that had been in the previous Presbyterian hymnal. The Presbyterian Committee on Congregational Song issued a statement explaining the rationale and process. The group wanted to keep the song but with a slight edit, so they requested permission from the copyright holders to change "the wrath of God was satisfied" to "the love of God was magnified" to better fit with theological understandings of the cross and the nature of God. However, after that request was rejected and they had to consider the hymn unaltered, the committee vote fell short of the two-thirds mark necessary for a song to make the cut.[15] Apparently, sufficient theological concerns did not arise about the Christian Nationalism embedded in multiple hymns.

Common Prayer

In addition to songs and sermons, Christian Nationalistic ideas can creep into worship in other ways. Sometimes the ideology can be found in the prayers and liturgies used. As an example, let's consider *The Book of Common Prayer* used for worship by the Episcopal Church. Tracing back hundreds of years, it represents a significant worship tradition. The latest version was revised in 1979 and includes nearly 1,000 pages of liturgies, prayers, lectionary passages, creeds, and the Psalter. Much of it offers biblical passages, prayers, and other liturgical suggestions for worship services. Attention is

---

[15] Jerry L. Van Mater, "Presbyterian Hymnal Producers Respond to Misinformation," PCUSA, August 9, 2013, https://www.pcusa.org/news/2013/8/9/presbyterian-hymnal-producers-respond-misinformati.

given to various seasons like Advent, Lent, Easter, and Pentecost. And there are suggested prayers for holy days, such as those honoring Saint Andrew (November 30), the Holy Innocents (December 28), the conversion of Saint Paul (January 25), Saint Mark (April 25), and Saint Mary Magdalene (July 22).

But one of the holy days is Independence Day, so there are also liturgies for that occasion. A prayer for July 4 reads:

> Lord God Almighty, in whose Name the founders of this country won liberty for themselves and for us, and lit the torch of freedom for nations then unborn: Grant that we and all the people of this land may have grace to maintain our liberties in righteousness and peace; through Jesus Christ our Lord, who lives and reigns with you and the Holy Spirit, one God, for ever and ever. Amen," reads a prayer for July 4.[16]

Elsewhere amid prayers for the church, global peace, prisoners, the poor, creation and conservation, families, and more, the book includes several prayers for aspects of national life. Like the prayer for the feast day of the Fourth of July, the prayers subtly embed ideas of the nation being intended as a Christian land with Christian leaders intentionally legislating on God's behalf:

> O Lord our Governor, whose glory is in all the world ... grant to the President of the United States, the Governor of this State (or Commonwealth), and to all in authority, wisdom, and strength to know and to do thy will. Fill them with the love of truth and righteousness, and make them ever mindful of their calling to serve this people in thy fear; through Jesus Christ our Lord, who liveth and reigneth with thee and the Holy Spirit, one God, world without end.[17]

Another prayer reads: "We beseech thee so to guide and bless our Senators and Representatives in Congress assembled (or in the Legislature of this State, or Commonwealth), that they may enact such laws as shall please thee, to the glory of thy Name and the welfare of this people; through Jesus Christ our Lord. Amen."[18]

---

[16] *The Book of Common Prayer: An Administration of the Sacraments and Other Rites and Ceremonies of the Church* (New York: Church Publishing Incorporated), 242.

[17] *The Book of Common Prayer*, 820.

[18] *The Book of Common Prayer*, 821.

Yet another prayer for the courts similarly calls on judges and justices to listen to God in their rulings: "Almighty God, who sittest in the throne judging right: We humbly beseech thee to bless the courts of justice and the magistrates in all this land; and give unto them the spirit of wisdom and understanding, that they may discern the truth, and impartially administer the law in the fear of thee alone; through him who shall come to be our Judge, thy Son our Savior Jesus Christ. Amen."[19] A prayer for an election asks God to lead the people—some of whom will listen to the prayer as it's offered to God during the service—to make wise decisions and vote for people who will ensure "our nation be enabled to fulfill your purposes; through Jesus Christ our Lord."[20] Another prayer requests divine protection for the U.S. Armed Forces and asks God to "defend them day by day with your heavenly grace."[21]

These prayers account for just a few pages in the massive volume. Numerous more prayers counter nationalistic tendencies by lifting up global concerns. The book is also full of prayers and readings emphasizing social justice issues as one would expect in an Episcopal congregation. There's even a tension in the lectionary passages that subtly shows the struggle of pushing the vision of a progressive, global faith while living in a culture that often acts as if God and country cannot be put asunder. The recommended lectionary readings for Independence Day include a passage in Hebrews 11 about being citizens of a better, heavenly country and Jesus's teaching in the Sermon on the Mount about loving one's enemies (a particularly helpful counter over the verses earlier in that chapter about a "city on a hill" that is commonly invoked in Christian Nationalistic ways). But an alternative slate of passages listed that could be used that day or an occasion "for the nation" includes Romans 13 about submitting to governmental authority, a teaching of Jesus about paying taxes, and a passage from Isaiah 26 about "the nation that keeps faith" and follows God. Those two sets of biblical passages could significantly alter the tone of a Fourth of July service (especially if a service using the latter texts also included patriotic hymns).

---

[19] *The Book of Common Prayer*, 821.
[20] *The Book of Common Prayer*, 822.
[21] *The Book of Common Prayer*, 823.

Given the options congregations have, there could be a wide difference between individual Episcopal services. Some congregations might skip over the more nationalistic sections completely while others might emphasize them. And while the nationalistic aspects remain a minor part of the liturgy, they're still there. Similar sprinklings could be found in the prayers, sermons, and other rituals in numerous other mainline congregations across the country over the past century. The question is: How much yeast of nationalism does it take to impact the whole loaf? Even working in a little Christian Nationalism can prime members to accept more extreme and dangerous forms now found in many evangelical sanctuaries and events.

The nationalism in *The Book of Common Prayer* is admittedly mild compared with older versions of the liturgy from the Church of England. The version the Episcopal Church adapted is less likely to bow before the state than that from the main Anglican branch that still enjoys the privilege of being an established state church. This was on display in May 2023 during the coronation of King Charles III. The liturgy used during the coronation included numerous Christian Nationalistic moments. Like when the king received a Bible to, as the minister who presented it said, "keep you ever mindful of the law and the gospel of God as the rule for the whole life and government of Christian Princes."[22] Or during the oath Charles took as he professed his Protestant faith and pledged to "maintain and preserve inviolably the settlement of the Church of England, and the doctrine, worship, discipline, and government thereof, as by law established in England." Or when the archbishop pledged the Church's homage to Charles as "our Sovereign Lord, Defender of the Faith." Christian Nationalism helped conceive the Church of England and remains in its DNA. It will take significant—and intentional—work to deprogram it.

This nationalistic flavor can be seen in the Bicentennial liturgy book published by the Episcopal Church, *This Nation Under God: A Book of Aids to Worship in the Bicentennial Year 1976*. After a number of prayers, liturgies, and suggested biblical passages for

[22] Brian Kaylor, "Coronating Christian Nationalism," *A Public Witness*, May 2, 2023, https://publicwitness.wordandway.org/p/coronating-christian-nationalism.

various services during the Bicentennial year, the book includes what a traditional service would have looked like in 1776 so that a congregation could reenact such liturgy on the Fourth of July. That means the liturgy comes from The *Book of Common Prayer* of 1662. Thus, as Episcopal churches would've in 1776, the liturgy includes references to England's king. As one litany offers:

> That it may please thee to keep and strengthen in the true worshipping of thee, in righteousness and holiness of life, thy Servant George, our most gracious King and Governour; We beseech thee to hear us, good Lord. ... That it may please thee to bless and preserve our gracious Queen Charlotte, their royal highnesses, George Prince of Wales, the Dowager Princess of Wales, and all the Royal Family; We beseech thee to hear us, good Lord.[23]

A pray for use during a communion service similarly reads:

> Almighty and everlasting God, we are taught by thy holy word, that the hearts of Kings are in thy rule and governance, and that thou dost dispose and turn them as it seemth best to thy godly wisdom. We humbly beseech thee so to dispose and govern the heart of George thy Servant, our King and Governour, that, in all his thoughts, words, and works, he may ever seek thy honour and glory, and study to preserve thy people committed to his charge, in wealth, peace, and godliness.[24]

And another prayer offers, "We beseech thee also to save and defend all Christian Kings, Princes, and Governours; and specially thy servant George our King; that under him we may be godly and quietly governed."[25]

We imagine those moments sounded odd when used for a bicentennial service in 1976. If only the Christian Nationalism of today also rang out as problematic.

---

[23] *This Nation Under God: A Book of Aids to Worship in the Bicentennial Year 1976* (New York: Seabury Press, 1976), 48.

[24] *This Nation Under God*, 53.

[25] *This Nation Under God*, 55.

The Martian Test

At the time of King Charles III's coronation, Stephen Backhouse, a lecturer in social and political theology at St. Mellitus College (an Anglican school in England), recommended using the "Martian test" when watching the coronation service: "If a Martian was watching the coronation service, you'd ask them what [they'd] learn about English religion. And they'd say, 'Well, it looks like they worship the king.' And I'd say, 'Yeah, you're right.'"[26]

We suggest a similar test when considering the Christian Nationalism long embedded in our worship services. When one grows up used to a certain way of doing things, it can seem natural. If one's family of birth fought every night, then one would grow up thinking all families act like that. That's a danger of the pervasiveness of Christian Nationalism. For those who grew up in White churches in the U.S.—mainline, evangelical, Pentecostal, or Catholic—Christian Nationalism was often in the air. We breathed it in, seeing it as inherently part of what it means to be Christian.

But what if Marvin the Martian showed up in a mainline service on the Fourth of July as he hunted for that rascally rabbit? Without any information about our religion, who or what would he think we worship? He'd surely catch the idea of Jesus. But we suspect he'd also see us worshiping the United States of America. Perhaps he'd offer some pithy complaint about this dual theology: "Earthlings have no sense of direction!" And while he ends a cartoonishly violent *Looney Tunes* episode with the reassuring line, "Don't worry folks; after all it's only a cartoon," after the Capitol insurrection we can't shrug off the violence of Christian Nationalism. We must pay more attention to what is contaminating our atmosphere.

---

[26] Madeleine Davies, "UK Coronation Remains Religious, Even if the Country Isn't," *Christianity Today*, May 2, 2023, https://www.christianitytoday.com/ct/2023/may-web-only/uk-king-charles-coronation-church-of-england-religious-mona.html.

Chapter 9

A BANNER DECISION

The fine Hilda Ramirez received totaled more than $300,000. As part of the Trump Administration's crackdown on immigrants living in the United States without documentation, U.S. Immigration and Customs Enforcement sent notices assessing individuals a penalty of $799 per day for not leaving the country.[1] While ICE eventually backed away from the harsh tactic, the assessments raised an obvious question: If the government knew where to send the letter about the fine, why couldn't it take action to remove Ramirez from the country?

It's because she and other immigrants had taken up residence inside churches, seeking sanctuary from immigration authorities. In Ramirez's case,[2] she found refuge at St. Andrew's Presbyterian Church, a PCUSA congregation in Austin, Texas.

This practice developed out of ancient traditions that sought to protect vulnerable people against abuses of state authority. Citing obligations to a power higher than human governments, medieval churches extended sanctuary to those perceived as being treated too harshly by earthly rulers for violating secular law. The provision

---

[1] Julián Aguilar, "Immigration Agency Decides Against Six-Figure Fines for Undocumented Immigrants Living in Sanctuaries," *Texas Tribune*, October 23, 2019, https://www.texastribune.org/2019/10/23/trump-administration-cancels-big-fines-some-undocumented-immigrants.

[2] The Biden Administration later allowed Ramirez and others to temporarily remain in the United States; see: Joel Rose, "Four Immigrants Who Sought Sanctuary in Churches No Longer Face Deportation," NPR, June 21, 2023, https://www.npr.org/2023/06/21/1183528143/four-immigrants-who-sought-sanctuary-in-churches-no-longer-face-deportation-fine.

of safety allowed the wrongdoer time to make amends to those
harmed and to find reconciliation with the community. If that was
not possible, they would be sent into exile.

A modern sanctuary movement formed in the United States
in the 1980s around the plight of refugees, especially those fleeing
violence in El Salvador and Guatemala. After more than a dozen
Salvadorans died crossing the Arizona desert and immigration
officials planned to deport the survivors back into the hands of an
oppressive government, churches began organizing to shelter the
persecuted migrants. Thousands of churches joined the effort over
the ensuing decade as the official policy of the U.S. government failed
to address the moral crisis.[3]

Another expression of this social witness has emerged with the
rise of anti-immigrant rhetoric and legislation since the mid-2000s.
Organizing under the banner of the "New Sanctuary Movement,"
hundreds of churches again sought to shelter vulnerable immigrants
and advocate for changes to government policy. Alexia Salvatierra,
an Evangelical Lutheran Church in America pastor and seminary
professor who has been at the forefront of the organizing efforts,
explained its power:

> Regarding the Sanctuary Movement, there are people in
> public sanctuary, living inside churches while we try to
> arrange assistance. One of the reasons for public sanctuary
> is the opportunity to tell their story. And the participation of
> non-immigrants standing with and suffering with someone
> in sanctuary encourages other citizens to take a second look
> and not accept the assumptions that immigrants are a threat
> or a drain, but to begin to see them as brothers and sisters.[4]

The election of Donald Trump and the immigration agenda pursued
by his administration brought renewed urgency and attention
to such sanctuary efforts. Many of the churches offering to take

---

[3] Mario Garcia, "More Central American Migrants Take Shelter in
Churches, Recalling 1980s Sanctuary Movement," *The Conversation*, July
30, 2019, https://theconversation.com/more-central-american-migrants-
take-shelter-in-churches-recalling-1980s-sanctuary-movement-120535.

[4] Sarah Quezada, "How Churches Can Give Sanctuary and Still
Support the Law," *Christianity Today*, March 17, 2017, https://www.
christianitytoday.com/ct/2017/march-web-only/how-churches-can-
give-sanctuary-to-immigrants-and-still-sup.html.

in undocumented immigrants facing deportation were mainline Protestant congregations mounting a religious witness against state policy.

"People are feeling more vulnerable than before," United Methodist pastor Robin Hynicka said about his congregation's efforts. "[But] people of faith and conscience are walking alongside the immigrant community. Sanctuary provides a moral alternative to what we think is an immoral policy."[5]

Despite their historical and contemporary use as a refuge for those sought after by law enforcement, church sanctuaries do not actually enjoy a privileged legal status in the United States. ICE designates them as a "protected area" where, according to guidelines issued in 2021, officers should "refrain from taking enforcement actions."[6] This policy can be easily changed by different administrations or ignored based on circumstances. Indeed, ICE agents arrested an asylum-seeker in the fall of 2020 on the grounds of a United Methodist church in Maryland where he and his wife lived and worked in support of the church's ministry. The violation of ICE's stated policy drew outrage and rebuke from religious leaders.

"As a bishop and adjudicatory leader I find this breach of established practice unconscionable," LaTrelle Easterling, the head of the United Methodist Church's Baltimore-Washington Conference and a former prosecutor, said. "The sanctity of our sacred spaces should never be violated, and this calls into question [the Trump] administration's respect for communities of faith and for God's people."[7]

What generally keeps authorities from breaking down church doors are not statutory prohibitions. In theory, religious communities

---

[5] Harriet Sherwood, "Hundreds of Churches Offer Sanctuary to Undocumented Migrants After Election," *The Guardian*, November 27, 2016, https://www.theguardian.com/us-news/2016/nov/27/undocumented-immigrations-us-churches-sanctuary-trump.

[6] "Protected Areas Enforcement Actions," U.S. Immigrations and Customs Enforcement, accessed September 25, 2023, https://www.ice.gov/about-ice/ero/protected-areas.

[7] Jack Jenkins, "ICE Apprehension on Church Grounds Violated Federal Policy, Say Faith Leaders," *Religion News Service,* September 21, 2020, https://religionnews.com/2020/09/21/ice-apprehension-on-church-grounds-violated-federal-policy-say-faith-leaders.

and their leaders could face legal repercussions themselves for providing refuge to those sought by law enforcement. Instead, it's a social norm that assigns a unique regard for the integrity of sacred spaces—and fear of the negative publicity that would arise from its violation—that makes practices of sanctuary possible.

You do not need to be a supporter of the sanctuary movement or hold a particular stance on immigration issues to understand the value of that respect. Places of religious worship are set apart by what happens inside of them. Traditional church architecture marks these buildings as serving a distinctive purpose. Christian theology highlights the obligations that adherents have to God that are over and above those claimed by human rulers. Worship spaces facilitate our connection to what is transcendent and alter how we interact with our temporary environments.

People seek sanctuary in churches because of the belief that such spaces are set apart from the world in an important way, with those who gather there holding obligations to something beyond human authorities. Given this long history of church sanctuaries existing as spaces beyond the government's claims, why do we use them to celebrate the nation? Specifically, why do so many churches place the U.S. flag in a place where the presence of the Lord who rules all the nations is thought to be near?

Does That Star-Spangled Banner Yet Wave?

In mainline, evangelical, Pentecostal, Catholic, and other congregations across the country, one similarity often found is the presence of the American flag. Sometimes it waves on a pole just outside the church, welcoming people to the building along with the name of the church and a sign that lists the pastor's name and perhaps the upcoming sermon title or a witty note. Other times, the flag stands inside the sanctuary, becoming part of the sacred architecture and discipling people in how to think about worship and following God. Since the American flag has often stood near the pulpit for decades, many accept its presence as just the way things should be. Having been baptized since birth into this design choice, many Christians—even those who abhor the Christian Nationalism on display in the Capitol insurrection—don't consider the problematic sermons preached by the flags in our sanctuaries.

How and why many churches started flying the flag is often unknown. As Lutheran scholar Benjamin Nickodemus explained, "There have never been any formal decisions made about doing so. There are no convention resolutions or any major studies written in any of Lutheran periodicals. Flag introduction came from the 'bottom up' and was driven by laity, thus there was no standard practice."[8] But like many of the Christian Nationalistic expressions we've explored, flags often moved into churches during times of war. The first wave came during the Civil War. With the nation—and churches—divided by the conflict, the flag became a way of marking one's loyalties. It even created conflict. For instance, historian Timothy Wesley recounted an incident in the border state of Missouri where Northern and Southern Methodists shared the same building.[9] One Sunday, the Southern Methodists arrived to find an American flag tacked to the pulpit from the Union-backing service. A minor scrimmage broke out after some Union supporters took the flag and held it over the door in hopes of forcing the Southern Methodist minister to walk underneath it. Flag conflicts continue in churches a century and a half later!

Zeal for the U.S. flag grew in American culture in the latter part of the nineteenth century, in part from the advocacy of Union veterans. Churches weren't exempt from such a movement. Rev. George Gue, a Methodist Episcopal minister who served as a Union chaplain during the war, compiled a book of poems and essays to honor the flag. Published in 1890 with about 150 pieces—several of them by ministers—Gue argued in the preface to *Our Country's Flag* that "in every schoolroom and over every pulpit this flag should be unfurled as an emblem of our Christian civilization and a lesson of patriotic devotion to all the intuitions of this great American republic."[10] In the book, he printed a resolution passed the previous year by the Central Illinois Conference of the Methodist Episcopal Church (which he was part of): "Resolved, that we, as a conference, do recommend that the American flag be placed in our churches and Sunday Schools as an emblem of our Christian civilization."[11]

---

[8] Benjamin J. Nickodemus, "The Unwaved Flag in Churches: The U.S. Flag in American Lutheran Church Sanctuaries," *Raven: A Journal of Vexillology* 28 (2021): 41.

[9] Timothy L. Wesley, *The Politics of Faith During the Civil War* (Baton Rouge: Louisiana State University Press, 2013).

[10] George W. Gue, *Our Country's Flag* (Davenport: Egbert, Fidlar, & Chambers, 1890), 5–6.

[11] Gue, *Our Country's Flag*, 95.

An essay in the book similarly pushed for churches to display the Stars and Stripes in churches for civic reasons:

Place the flag in the churches of our country, for is not the love of country next to that of God? There, in association with the church, let it remain constantly before the eye; then our voters will be influenced, through the preaching of the truth in connection with this symbol of purity and valor, to see in a truer and more reverential light the vastness of the responsibility devolving upon them in their duty to the government. When casting their votes the apparition of the church and flag will appear, and they will say: "I am an American, and to be true I must take my stand for the glory of God, the protection of home, and the highest good of my native land."[12]

A poem in the book honoring the "spirit of 1861" encouraged people to fly the flag "from church, from fort, from housetop, o'er the city, on the seas" and asked God to "bless our banner" and watch over the nation.[13]

Another page in the book includes a single quote attributed to Rev. E. A. Anderson in 1861: "Let the flag of our country wave from the spire of every church in the land, with nothing above it save the cross of Christ."[14] A poem, "Our Country's Flag on God's Sacred Altars" by James W. Temple, was one Gue mentioned he requested be written for the book. Temple wrote:

Where altars to our Maker rise,
There let his standards greet the skies;
And to heaven's welcoming breezes fling
The banners of our Lord, the King!
... God of the saints! Land of the free!
Let thy fair banners blended be!
And o'er heaven's sacred altars wave
The flag that guards the free and brave![15]

---

[12] Lizzie T. Gassett, "The Flag of the United States," in Gue, *Our Country's Flag*, 42.

[13] H.E.T., "Our Star-Gemmed Banner—Spirit of 1861," in Gue, *Our Country's Flag*, 90.

[14] E.A. Anderson, "The Flag Over Our Churches," in Gue, *Our Country's Flag*, 100.

[15] James W. Temple, "Our Country's Flag on God's Sacred Altars," in Gue, *Our Country's Flag*, 93.

Other pieces in the book joined the crusade for Old Glory in their local congregations.

World War I brought more flags into sanctuaries, especially among Lutheran and other German immigrant congregations. Those who didn't fly the flag could face threats and acts of violence amid allegations they supported the Kaiser. However, nationalistic fervor also led non-immigrant congregations to put up flags. Around the same time, some Klansmen encouraged churches to display the flag, calling it a heavenly gift along with the Bible.[16] Nickodemus documented that among Lutheran churches the American flag often started flying along with a service flag. Many people would raise a service flag at home during the Great War with a star for every family member serving in uniform. Churches were encouraged to fly such flags with stars for its members in military service—but the flags were in the parish hall or vestibule, not the sanctuary. After the war, "the service flags were removed, the American flags remained."[17]

During the 1930s, American flags increasingly moved from other places in a church building into the sanctuary. But an action by Congress amid another world war increased the problems with such messaging. Although a group of civic organizations led by the American Legion had in 1923 developed guidelines for honoring and displaying the U.S. flag, Congress officially adopted a Flag Code in 1942 barely six months after the bombing of Pearl Harbor. In addition to addressing the Pledge and how to salute the flag, it prescribed rules for properly flying the flag in relation to other banners. With many congregations already flying the American flag and the Christian flag (which we'll address more in a moment), following the Flag Code was the patriotic thing to do during a time of war. But the government's rules brought significant theological implications. The Flag Code sought to ensure the U.S. flag would "hold the position of superior prominence." This means flying it on top of a pole with other flags or in front of a line of flags being marched in somewhere. And it means, as the Flag Code instructs, "in the position of honor at the clergyman's or speaker's right as he faces the audience" with "any other flag so displayed ... placed on

---

[16] Thomas Kidd, "The Church and the American Flag," The Gospel Coalition, June 20, 2016, https://www.thegospelcoalition.org/blogs/evangelical-history/the-church-and-the-american-flag.

[17] Nickodemus, "The Unwaved Flag in Churches," 43.

the left of the clergyman or speaker or to the right of the audience." Accordingly, most churches that fly both American and Christian flags put Old Glory to the pastor's right (or the higher place on the flagpole) in "the position of superior prominence." That means they aren't just offering a kind of two kingdoms theology, acknowledging citizenship obligations to both an early and heavenly realm. Rather, the congregations symbolically say which kingdom they really follow, and which they find subservient or secondary at best.

While the presence of the American flag in a church today seems common, international visitors often find it surprising. One who wrote about his shock at seeing "the display of the American flag in churches" was German theologian Dietrich Bonhoeffer.[18] In 1939, he visited the U.S. (after having studied in New York City years earlier at Union Theological Seminary). He didn't stay long as he felt the need to return to his homeland and continue preaching against Adolf Hitler during a time when Nazi flags were draped on church altars—and he lost his life for such resistance. But as he reflected on issues of church and state in the U.S., the display of the American flag in churches struck him as a problem. He called it "a surprising custom in the land of church-state separation." While a U.S. flag in a sanctuary is less problematic than a Nazi one, any effort to raise a single country's banner in a church risks becoming nationalistic idolatry.

Even if it's not placed in "the position of superior prominence," bringing the American flag into the sanctuary sends the wrong message about God's love for—and our commitments to— our global neighbors. That's why numerous Christian bodies recommend against the practice. The U.S. Conference of Catholic Bishops encourages priests "not to place the flag within the sanctuary itself, in order to reserve that space for the altar" and other holy objects.[19] The United Methodist Church also recommends against it, noting it doesn't seem possible to both follow the U.S. Flag Code and properly

---

[18] Dietrich Bonhoeffer, "Protestantism Without Reformation," in Clifford J. Green and Michael P. DeJonge, eds., *The Bonhoeffer Reader* (Minneapolis: Fortress Press, 2013), 585.

[19] "Display of Flags in Catholic Churches," United States Conference of Bishops, https://www.usccb.org/prayer-and-worship/sacred-art-and-music/architecture-and-environment/display-of-flags-in-catholic-churches.

give the cross the place of higher allegiance. Their resource adds, "An American flag used in the worship of the universal church is no more appropriate than hanging a cross in a civil courtroom used by Americans of all religions."[20] The UMC added in another document, "Can the flag, which to many symbolizes economic and military might, stand near the cross with its meanings of humility, servanthood, and selfless sacrifice? Does 'Old Glory' in the congregation's place of worship conflict with the glorification of our unbounded, nationless God? Can the prophetic word—and even God's word of judgment—to a nation be heard when that nation's flag stands in a place of honor?"[21] Yet, despite this, a survey in 2009 found that 91% of UMC churches had an American flag on their premises, with 84% of them in the sanctuary.[22] We suspect many other denominations outside the historic peace churches (like the Mennonite Church USA) would similarly find a large number of congregations with the Stars and Stripes.

With research showing that the presence of a flag "fosters nationalist views in those exposed to it,"[23] pastors and church leaders should rethink the messages sent by the presence of the flag in a sanctuary during worship. As Winston Churchill put it, "We shape our buildings, and afterwards our buildings shape us." We reap what we sow. For decades, mainline and other churches have baptized the American flag as a holy symbol for use in worship, thus discipling generations of Christians in a faith that subtly but powerfully connects Christianity and nationalism.

---

[20] "Should We Have Flags in the Church? The Christian Flag and the American Flag," Discipleship Ministries, https://www.umcdiscipleship.org/resources/should-we-have-flags-in-the-church-the-christian-flag-and-the-american-flag.

[21] Karen Westerfield Tucker, "The American Flag in Methodist Worship: A Historical Look at Practice," Discipleship Ministries, 2002, https://www.umcdiscipleship.org/articles/the-american-flag-in-methodist-worship-a-historical-look-at-practice.

[22] Carrie Madren, "Should Star-Spangled Banner be in Church?" *Interpreter*, July-August 2010, https://web.archive.org/web/20120602191651/http://www.umc.org/site/apps/nlnet/content.aspx?c=lwL4KnN1LtH&b=4776577&ct=8491195&notoc=1.

[23] Markus Kemmelmeir and David G. Winter, "Sowing Patriotism, But Reaping Nationalism?: Consequences of Exposure to the American Flag," *Political Psychology* 29, no. 6 (2008), https://doi.org/10.1111/j.1467-9221.2008.00670.x.

Whither the Christian Flag?

Of course, there's another flag often flying with the U.S. flag in church sanctuaries or flagpoles: the Christian flag. It also showed up in the pro-Trump mob that violently stormed the U.S. Capitol. That's not the only time it's been co-opted for an ungodly agenda. Thus, it's worth considering whether we should keep it when we remove Old Glory from our churches. To consider what that means, we should go back to the beginning, with another story about some mainline Protestants.

The design of the Christian flag occurred in 1897. As the story goes, when a guest speaker failed to show up for Sunday School at the Coney Island Congregational Church (also known as Brighton Chapel) in Brooklyn, New York, a local leader gave an impromptu speech. Noticing an American flag draped over the corner of the pulpit, Charles Overton used the flag[24] as "his text." Overton then imagined aloud to his audience what a Christian flag might look like. The final product is quite similar to the Stars and Stripes that Overton chose as his "inspiration" (which seems like an even worse idea than using Leviticus for a sermon text). Simply remove the red stripes and white stars, and add a red cross inside the blue box. A week after Overton's "message," he draped a version of his Christian flag on the pulpit along with the American flag. That display served as the prototype for what is now generally called the Christian flag.

A few years later, the flag received a boost from famed songwriter Fanny Crosby, the Methodist Episcopal layperson who wrote more than 8,000 hymns and gospel songs. In 1903, she penned "The Christian Flag, Behold It," to honor the new banner:

Now throw it to the breeze,
And may it wave triumphant
O'er land and distant seas,
Till all the wide creation
Upon its folds shall gaze,
And all the world united,
Our loving Savior praise.[25]

---

[24] Ralph E. Diffendorfer, *Missionary Education in Home and School* (New York: Abingdon Press, 1917).

[25] https://hymnary.org/text/the_christian_flag_behold_it.

While the song didn't take off, a pledge did. In 1908, Rev. Lynn Harold Hough was inspired during a meeting at which a speaker talked about Overton's flag. Hough unveiled the pledge for use at a Christmas Eve service in 1908 at his church, Third Methodist Episcopal Church in Long Island City, New York. As with the design of the flag, this American minister borrowed from the U.S. counterpart for inspiration.

"I pledge allegiance to my flag and the Savior for whose kingdom it stands; one brotherhood uniting all mankind in service and love," Hough offered as the pledge.[26]

After the U.S. Pledge changed in 1923 from "allegiance to my flag" to "allegiance to the flag of the United States of America," the Christian flag pledge similarly changed from "my flag" to "the flag." Additionally, some today say "all Christians" or "all true Christians" instead of "all mankind." A version that circulates in some conservative churches declares, "I pledge allegiance to the Christian flag, and to the Savior for whose kingdom it stands; one Savior, crucified, risen, and coming again with life and liberty to all who believe." Regardless of the version, the use of the Christian flag and a pledge remain common at Vacation Bible Schools and other church moments geared towards children. As the creation of a song and pledge suggests, the use of the flag quickly took off. This popularity, however, also sparked questions of protocol—especially when rumors of war began to swirl.

Methodist minister Ralph Diffendorfer, who helped Overton popularize the Christian flag, insisted in 1917 that the banner should be a symbol of unity and peace. He explained: "The Christian flag bears no symbol of warfare or conquest. ... It stands for no creed nor denomination, but for Christianity. It is a banner of the Prince of Peace, and the Christian patriot who salutes it pledges allegiance to the Kingdom of God."[27] Crosby similarly sang an appeal for people to "unfurl it" to "bear the message, goodwill and peace to men."

In light of this background and faced with the looming threat of war, uncomfortable questions began to arise about the allegiance of Christians who waved it. Rev. James Russell Pollock, a young Methodist minister serving his first church in 1938, placed a new

---

[26] Diffendorfer, *Missionary Education in Home and School*, 184.

[27] Diffendorfer, *Missionary Education in Home and School*, 185.

Christian flag in the place of prominence in the sanctuary off to the pulpit's right and moved the American flag to the left. That symbolically showed allegiance to the Christian kingdom coming before obligations to one's earthly country. During the week after Pollock's redecorating, someone switched the placement of the U.S. and Christian flags—an action he attributed to people overreacting as news from Europe had people expecting war soon. In response, Pollock, who would soon serve as a chaplain in World War II, created his own code to justify his placement.[28] In his code, the Christian flag precedes all other flags (but follows the cross if they are both part of a processional), and the Christian flag dips to no other flags (but may dip to a cross at the altar). Additionally, the Christian flag should fly at the top position on a pole and maintain the position of honor when displayed together (such as to the preacher's right when on stage, or from the congregation's perspective that would mean off to the left of the pulpit). For Pollock, this code wasn't merely theological; it also represented his belief in the U.S. as a Christian nation.

The month after Japan bombed Pearl Harbor and brought the U.S. officially into World War II, the Christian flag came up for conversation at a January 23, 1942, meeting of the Federal Council of Churches (the main forerunner to the National Council of Churches). As the story often goes,[29] the council adopted the flag and therefore gave it an authoritative status. But the actual minutes from the meeting instead offer some warnings.

The Federal Council of Churches noted a few examples of "Christian" flags, and acknowledged Overton's design as "the form most generally regarded as the Christian flag."[30] But the resolution didn't actually adopt it. The council insisted it wasn't "attempting to prescribe regulations" but just offering "advice to churches" after having "received overtures and inquiries concerning the appropriate

---

[28] James R. Pollock, *The Christian Flag Code: Christ Above All*, 1981.

[29] See for instance: Robert P. Jones, "Despite White Christianity's Role in Capitol Assault, Some Signs of Hope and Chance," *Religion News Service*, July 16, 2021, https://religionnews.com/2021/07/16/despite-white-christianitys-disturbing-role-in-the-us-capitol-assault-there-are-signs-of-change; and Kimberly Winston, "The History Behind the Christian Flags Spotted at the Pro-Trump U.S. Capitol 'Coup,'" *Religion Unplugged*, January 6, 2021, https://religionunplugged.com/news/2021/1/6/some-history-behind-the-christian-flags-at-the-pro-trump-capitol-coup.

[30] *Federal Council Bulletin, volumes 25-27* (New York: Federal Council of the Churches of Christ in America, 1942), 11.

use and position of flags within the sanctuary." At a moment when many were thinking about waving flags at the start of a war, the Federal Council of Churches resolution offered caution about ultimate allegiance.

"The cross itself is generally accepted as a good and sufficient symbol for the house of God in the Christian tradition, without the use of a church flag," the resolution offered. "If a flag or banner representing the loyalty of the church to its head is used along with the flag of the nation in the sanctuary, the symbol of loyalty to God should have the place of highest honor."

So the Federal Council of Churches actually recommended the use of just a cross. And the council followed Pollock's ordering if a Christian flag appears along with the U.S. flag by outlining in the resolution where the flags should stand in relation to each other. Despite these efforts, Overton's Christian flag shows up in church sanctuaries throughout the country, usually positioned to the left of the preacher and therefore in a subservient position to the U.S. flag on the right.

A danger of creating symbols is losing control over their use. They can send different and even conflicting messages than what their creators originally intended—like we saw on January 6, 2021. As insurrectionists violently stormed the U.S. Capitol, the crowd carried a number of symbols to explain their loyalties and ideologies. Flying alongside numerous Trump flags were Confederate and Christian flags. Overton's symbol for everyone—the flag Diffendorfer called a banner of peace—was employed as a symbol for a partisan group bent on undermining American democracy. Many commentators correctly noted the presence of Christian flags as a sign of the White Christian Nationalism that helped fuel the mob. We suggest the problem is even worse than that. The insurrection also shows us that White supremacists are clearly adopting the Christian flag as their own, changing its meaning and denying its fundamental message that "Jesus is Lord." In fact, we're seeing in recent years the use of the Christian flag as a companion or even a stand-in banner for the Confederate battle flag. Consider a few examples:

- During a 2015 pro-Confederate flag rally at Stone Mountain in Georgia pushing back against demands that the Confederacy's banner be taken down in various public spaces, some of those present also waved Christian flags as a symbol they found compatible with the Confederate battle flag.[31]

- Also in 2015, a local member of the Sons of Confederate Veterans in Harleyville, South Carolina, told the *Post and Courier* the week after the Mother Emanuel shooting that he rotates flying a Confederate flag, Christian flag, yellow Gadsden flag, and state flag.[32]

- In that same year, a group that installs Confederate flags in Virginia replaced one in Danville at Christmas time with a Christian flag to accompany a nativity scene at the base of the pole.[33]

- In 2018, the *Richmond Free Press* published a photo of a Confederate flag flying in a city-owned cemetery with the headline "Why Is This flying?" The flag in question was erected and owned by the United Daughters of the Confederacy. The flag was replaced a few days later, apparently by the UDC, with a Christian flag.[34]

- After NASCAR banned Confederate flags in 2020, a racetrack owner in North Carolina announced a "heritage night" to "protect the sport we love." He advertised it as a time to come "purchase your Confederate flags and caps here, along with your Christian flag, American flag, Donald Trump flag and caps."[35]

---

[31] "Photos: Confederate Flag Rally at Stone Mountain Park," *Atlanta Journal-Constitution*, August 1, 2015, https://www.ajc.com/news/photos-confederate-flag-rally-stone-mountain-park/QP7NWbECMqiqZm4nBm4NYI.

[32] Brenda Rindge, "On Front Porches, Some Still Divided on Confederate Flag," *Charleston Post and Courier*, June 27, 2025, https://www.postandcourier.com/archives/on-front-porches-some-still-divided-on-confederate-flag/article_aedcd4ef-bdb9-5e69-9bab-0481ce8d0c65.html.

[33] Valerie Bragg, "City, Flaggers Meet About Confederate Flag Poles," WSET, December 16, 2015, https://wset.com/news/local/city-flaggers-meet-about-confederate-flag-poles.

[34] Jeremy M. Lazarus, "Confederate Flag Replaced at Riverview Cemetery," *Richmond Free Press*, April 13, 2018, https://richmondfreepress.com/news/2018/apr/13/confederate-flag-replaced-riverview-cemetery.

[35] Biba Adams, "NC Governor, Activists Condemn Speedway Owner Who Posted 'Bubba Rope' for Sale," *The Grio*, June 26, 2020, https://thegrio.com/2020/06/26/nc-governor-condemn-bubba-rope-for-sale.

- Also in 2020, a local Sons of Confederate Veterans group in Burke County, North Carolina, briefly replaced a large and controversial Confederate flag with U.S. and Christian flags on a flag pole that flies prominently above Interstate 40. The replacements flew during the two months just before the presidential election, then switched back to a Confederate flag.[36]

- In 2021, the reinterment service for Confederate Lieutenant General, slave trader, and Grand Wizard of the KKK Nathan Bedford Forrest and his wife, Mary, included draping his coffin with the Confederate flag and hers with the Christian flag (even though it wasn't created until after their deaths). One leader of the Sons of Confederate Veterans called the internment "a remarkable event" for "one of our heroes."[37] Even the rain on that day, he added, "was like God was crying, but then the rains, the tears, stopped and gave him the welcome home like it should be."

Such back-and-forth swapping between the flags occurs because of claims by defenders of the Confederate battle flag that it is a "Christian" symbol for what they believe is a "Christian" nation. With White supremacists needing more palatable symbols amid a backlash to Confederate imagery, we will likely see an increased effort to co-opt Christian symbols like Overton's flag to convey these ugly messages. In these moments, the flags are flown to make a statement. They are acts of defiance, plain and simple. We should not mistake the replacement of one flag for another as a gesture of contrition that indicates repentance. The underlying beliefs of the ones hoisting the banner remain unchanged.

So as we watch White supremacists claiming the Christian flag as their own symbol to complement or even stand in for a Confederate emblem, we remember a warning of history: Symbols

---

[36] "Group Raises Massive Confederate Flag Over I-40 Following Presidential Election," WSOC, November 10, 2020, https://www.wsoctv.com/news/local/group-raises-massive-confederate-flag-over-i-40-following-election/AGFAVL7JWFB5PCX665WWELWZH4.

[37] Mike Christen, "'Bringing Him Home': Nathan Bedford Forrest Gravesite Faces Birthplace, Chapel Hill, Tennessee," *Columbia Daily Herald*, September 25, 2021, https://www.columbiadailyherald.com/story/news/2021/09/26/nathan-bedford-forrest-rests-facing-his-native-chapel-hill/5793143001.

don't necessarily keep the meaning intended by their creators. For instance, the swastika is an ancient symbol dating back to at least the time of King David that has held religious meaning for Buddhists, Hindus, and other eastern Asian religions. Then the Nazi regime co-opted the symbol, transforming it into a deplorable emblem of White supremacy, anti-Semitism, and vile hatred. Moving in the other direction, early Christians adopted a symbol of torture and death—the cross—because Jesus's death and resurrection gave it new meanings of forgiveness and love, victory, and liberation. It is the holiness of that symbol and its central meaning to our faith as followers of the crucified servant that should inspire us to protect its sacred meaning. This emerging trend that hijacks powerful Christian imagery and imbues it with connotations of hatred should be abhorrent to all who place their ultimate loyalty in Christ.

We're not particularly fans of Overton's overly American design for the Christian flag. We're troubled when church sanctuaries display the symbol in ways suggesting, however inadvertently, that the kingdom of God is subservient to a human nation. From our perspective, the Federal Council of Churches got it right in 1942 when they recommended focusing on the cross over the flag. Still, what worries us even more is when White supremacists seem bent on turning the Christian flag, the cross stitched upon it, or any Christian symbols into banners for their ideology. We must speak out when we see Christian flags employed alongside Confederate flags like at the January 6 insurrection or at a funeral service commemorating Confederate leaders, or when people act like the Christian flag is a perfect substitute for a Confederate banner on a flagpole. If Christians don't criticize these moments and contest the efforts to hijack sacred imagery, we will continue to see our treasured symbols used with hostile intents. As the Apostle Paul wrote, he was called to keep preaching the gospel "lest the cross of Christ be emptied of its power" (1 Corinthians 1:17). In this moment, that call to faithful vigilance and persistence belongs to us all. The stakes are too high to wave the white flag.

Section IV

LIVING IN THE NATION
MAINLINE PROTESTANTS BUILT

Chapter 10

FAILED STATE

Moments after Rep. Mike Johnson from Louisiana was elected as speaker of the U.S. House of Representatives on October 25, 2023, he offered his acceptance remarks from the chamber's podium. A little-known congressman with the least experience of anyone elected speaker in 140 years, Johnson's speech gave him the opportunity to introduce himself to the nation. A Southern Baptist layman who had served in denominational roles as he built a career working for conservative Christian law firms, Johnson quickly defined himself in religious terms. In fact, he even suggested God had made him the new speaker.

"I don't believe there are any coincidences in a matter like this," he declared. "I believe that Scripture, the Bible is very clear that God is the one that raises up those in authority. He raised up each of you, all of us. And I believe that God has ordained and allowed each one of us to be brought here for this specific moment in this time."[1]

With a long record of espousing Christian Nationalism,[2] Johnson also argued the U.S. should be viewed as a Christian country. After saying that the lawmakers had been chosen by God and should serve God in their position, Johnson pointed out that behind him on the House chamber wall it read "In God We Trust." He mentioned the phrase had been etched in the wall in 1962.

---

[1] "U.S. House of Representatives Session, Part 1," C-SPAN, October 25, 2023, https://www.c-span.org/video/?531374-1/house-session-part-1.

[2] Brian Kaylor and Jeremy Fuzy, "Christian Nationalism in the Speaker's Chair," *A Public Witness*, October 26, 2023, https://publicwitness.wordandway.org/p/christian-nationalism-in-the-speakers.

"These words were placed here above us, this motto was placed here as a rebuke of the Cold War-era philosophy of the Soviet Union. That philosophy was Marxism and communism, which begins with the premise that there is no God. This is a critical distinction," Johnson added as he insisted America had been founded on "a creed."

Johnson also emphasized the national motto in his first social media post after his election, which was a picture of "In God We Trust" above the U.S. flag in the House chamber.[3] But while Johnson got the year right in his history lesson about "In God We Trust" in the House chamber, he messed up a key part of the reason. By now you know this story involves mainline Protestants. Yet, it came in 1962 not simply because of the Soviet Union but because of a more domestic issue: the U.S. Supreme Court's ruling against government-written prayers in public schools. As we noted back in chapter 2, prayer in New York schools came with the endorsement of mainline Protestant clergy as they built Christian Nationalism. Returning prayer to public schools is an issue that animates those pushing the ideology today. And it drew the attention of mainline Protestants in Congress immediately after the justices made their landmark ruling.

Thirty-seven days after the ruling in *Engel v. Vitale* against coercive government prayers in public schools, Democratic Rep. Fred Marshall of Minnesota introduced a bill to remove some of the gold stars on the House wall behind the speaker's podium and instead put "In God We Trust" in gold letters. After a review of the proposal with the architect of the Capitol, lawmakers unanimously passed it on September 27. Before they did so, Marshall made the case for his resolution. The Methodist layman argued that installing "the words 'In God We Trust' would be a reminder to all of us and would reaffirm our faith in God."[4] Marshall added:

> During the times when our country is facing great crises, it is well that we remind ourselves of our reliance upon God and reaffirm our faith in him. I hope that the House will unanimously adopt this resolution and when members read the wording they will be inspired to greater faith. It

[3] Speaker Mike Johnson (@SpeakerJohnson), October 25, 2023, https://twitter.com/RepMikeJohnson/status/1717194879116148974.

[4] *Congressional Record, Proceeding and Debates of the 87th Congress, Second Volume* 198 (1962): 21100.

will be a constant reminder to visitors in the chamber of this country's faith in the words "In God We Trust."

Democratic Rep. William Randall of Missouri (who was also a Methodist) praised the resolution after its unanimous passage. He lamented the "omission" of the phrase thus far from the chamber and expressed "wonderment as to why all of us so long neglected" to make the change Marshall had proposed.[5] He recounted some of the history of the phrase appearing on U.S. money as proof that the phrase should be put in the chamber.

"Hereafter, we are to have continuously before our eyes our recognition of Almighty God and that our faith, trust, and hope are reposed in his goodness," Randall argued, adding that the resolution's passage had "emphasized anew that we are not only a God-fearing people but that we all realize that only by faith and trust in God can there be any hope for the solution of what seems to be the endless problems facing the Congress in world affairs and within our country."[6]

Randall also invoked high court's recent school prayer decision:

One of the byproducts of our act today is that we have given perhaps not directly but yet in a not-so-subtle way our answer to the recent decision of the U.S. Supreme Court order banning the regent's prayer from the New York State schools. At the conclusion of the session, some members were heard to say that we had just reversed the decision of the Supreme Court. They may be right, but this we know: that our action of today will go a long way to reaffirm the faith of every member in our heavenly Father by the constant reminder of our national motto, "In God We Trust."[7]

Randall admitted that putting God in the chamber was an attempt to brand the nation religiously after the Supreme Court—as those who push Christian Nationalism often put it—had kicked God out of schools. He also insisted it represented the Christian faith of every member of the U.S. House, thus civically excommunicating those of different religious beliefs as neither fully American nor loyal leaders

---

[5] *Congressional Record*, 21101.
[6] *Congressional Record*, 21101–21102.
[7] *Congressional Record*, 21102.

of the nation. Six decades later, Speaker Johnson pointed to the same words to do essentially the same thing as he espoused his beliefs that the nation is intended to be Christian and its elected members are to be servants of God's will (instead of representatives of the people following the Constitution).

While journalists, commentators, and progressive clergy quickly pointed to Johnson's remarks as more proof of his Christian Nationalism, the primary evidence the conservative evangelical House leader had mustered up came from what mainline Protestants had literally constructed in the House chamber. That holds true in many other debates today where evangelical politicians and preachers push for government backing of their religious tradition. As they claim the U.S. is a "Christian nation," the proof they point to is often the things we have covered in this book that mainline Protestants accomplished. From legislating prayer in public schools to storming the Capitol on January 6, 2021, inspiration has been derived in the present from the work of mainline Protestants in the past. Such unintended consequences haunt us today. When it comes to church-state debates, we're living in the political timeline mainline Protestants established.

Oklahoma!

In June 2023, the Oklahoma Statewide Virtual Charter School Board approved the nation's first religious public school. The St. Isidore of Seville Catholic Virtual School, run by the Archdiocese of Oklahoma City, achieved that designation after months of lobbying from proponents and critics. Earlier in the process, Republican state Attorney General John O'Connor issued an opinion claiming that even though Oklahoma law prohibited charter schools from being sectarian, he believed the prohibition was unconstitutional and thus it would be okay for the state to create publicly-funded sectarian charter schools. O'Connor, who is Catholic, issued his opinion while a lame duck and thus was out of office by the time the state board actually heard the proposal in early 2023. He had been appointed to the AG spot in 2021 following a resignation and then he lost the Republican primary as he sought to keep the job.

Shortly after the archdiocese officially presented its proposal, the man who defeated O'Connor withdrew his predecessor's opinion.

Gentner Drummond, also a Republican, argued that O'Connor had not followed proper procedures and should not have released the opinion. Additionally, Drummond said his predecessor's opinion "misuses the concept of religious liberty by employing it as a means to justify state-funded religion."[8] The new AG added he was "not currently comfortable advising" the board to violate the state Constitution.

While the state's new Republican AG warned against the proposal, the state's new Republican superintendent of public instruction (also an elected position), Ryan Walters, started pushing for more Christian Nationalism in public schools, including his support for the Catholic charter school. After lawmakers in neighboring Texas failed to pass a bill to mandate posting the Ten Commandments in every public school classroom, Walters called on Oklahoma to require that display of sectarian beliefs as well. When the time came to vote on the Catholic school, the state board backed it 3-2, thus siding with Walters in his goal of bringing more Christianity into the state's school system. The decision quickly sparked a rebuke from the state's AG.

"The approval of any publicly funded religious school is contrary to Oklahoma law and not in the best interest of taxpayers," Drummond said. "It's extremely disappointing that board members violated their oath in order to fund religious schools with our tax dollars. In doing so, these members have exposed themselves and the state to potential legal action that could be costly."[9]

It didn't take long for Drummond's prophecy to be fulfilled. The next month a group of clergy, public school parents, and public education advocates sued the state.

"Charter schools are public schools, not Sunday Schools," said Rachel Laser, president and CEO of Americans United for Separation of Church and State (one of the organizations supporting the

---

[8] Gentner Drummond, "RE: Attorney General Opinion 2022-7," February 23, 2023, https://www.oag.ok.gov/sites/g/files/gmc766/f/documents/2023/rebecca_wilkinson_ag_opinion_2022-7_virtual_charter_schools.pdf.

[9] "Drummond Says Religious Charter School Approval Is Unconstitutional," Office of the Oklahoma Attorney General, June 5, 2023, https://www.oag.ok.gov/articles/drummond-says-religious-charter-school-approval-unconstitutional.

plaintiffs) as she announced the litigation on July 31. "A religious public school is a contradiction in terms and a clear violation of Oklahoma law."[10]

"A religious public charter school betrays our country's promises of church-state separation and inclusive public education," she added. "We're bringing today's lawsuit to protect the religious freedom of Oklahoma public school families and taxpayers, and to stop Christian Nationalists from taking over our public schools across the nation."

As the state's AG had argued, the lawsuit accused the state board of violating the state Constitution, the Oklahoma Charter Schools Act, and the board's own regulations. The lawsuit also insisted that the idea of a sectarian public charter school runs counter to the vision of public education. The lawsuit explains:

> The defining feature of America's public schools is that they must welcome and serve all students, regardless of a student's background, beliefs, or abilities. Oklahoma embraces this core principle in its constitution and through a comprehensive system of statutes and regulations. Schools that do not adhere to this principle have long existed and are entitled to operate, but they cannot be part of the public-education system. Permitting otherwise would upend the legal framework Oklahoma has constructed to govern public schools and protect students.[11]

Some clergy added their names and voices to the effort as plaintiffs, pushing back against the claim that advocating for church-state separation is a mission solely for the godless. For instance, Lori Walke, the senior minister at Mayflower Congregational United Church of Christ in Oklahoma City, explained that as a UCC pastor and lawyer she cares "deeply about religious freedom" and thus joined the effort to sue the Sooner State.

"It is difficult to overstate how important the separation of church and state is to me," she said. "It is foundational to our state

---

[10] Brian Kaylor, "Lawsuit Schools Oklahoma on Church & State," *A Public Witness*, July 31, 2023, https://publicwitness.wordandway.org/p/lawsuit-schools-oklahoma-on-church.

[11] Kaylor, "Lawsuit Schools Oklahoma on Church & State."

and our country because it protects religious freedom for all of us. It ensures each of us can live out our conscience's dictates."[12]

Walke added:

> But creating a religious public charter school is not religious freedom. Forcing taxpayers to fund a religious school that, as they openly admit, will be a "place of evangelization" for one specific religion is not religious freedom. Diverting scarce public education resources to a religious school that can and will discriminate against children, families, and staff is not religious freedom. ... True religious freedom requires separation of church and state, and our democracy requires public education that is open to all.

This vision of church-state separation that protects true religious liberty for all is under attack across the country by those espousing Christian Nationalism—precisely because the historic principle stands in the way. As constitutional lawyer Andrew Seidel, American United's vice president of strategic communications and author of *American Crusade: How the Supreme Court is Weaponizing Religious Freedom*, explained, "seeking a Christian nation" is "fundamentally opposed" to church-state separation.[13] Thus, he invoked the "wall of separation between church and state" metaphor that Thomas Jefferson used in a letter to Baptists in 1802. Those pushing Christian Nationalism, Seidel explained, "don't get that if we build up that wall."

"The separation of church and state is the cure for Christian Nationalism in the United States," he added. "They cannot get what they want if there is a separation of church and state, if that wall between the two is tall and strong."

The words and writings of Jefferson, James Madison, and other U.S. founders in support of church-state separation undermine the false claims that the country was intended to be a "Christian" nation. Maintaining a robust church-state separation will go a long way in preventing more substantial efforts by those pushing Christian Nationalism to give special privileges to members of their own

---

[12] Kaylor, "Lawsuit Schools Oklahoma on Church & State."

[13] Brian Kaylor, "Seeking a Recommitment to Church-State Separation," *A Public Witness*, April 25, 2023, https://publicwitness. wordandway.org/p/seeking-a-recommitment-to-church.

faith at the expense of others. Speaker Johnson proves this desire to discredit church-state separation.

"I think we're a Christian nation. We certainly began that way,"[14] he declared during a sermon as he claimed—complete with a false quote attributed to President John Quincy Adams—that the founders created the U.S. to be Christian.

During a similar talk at another church, Johnson said he believes Thomas Jefferson—a man who literally cut out the miracles of Jesus from the New Testament—"was divinely inspired to write" the Declaration of Independence.[15] Johnson added that the founders broke away from England because they read the Bible and wanted to create a nation based on "this revolutionary idea that we owe our allegiance to the King of kings." As alleged proof of that claim, he pointed to the fourth verse of "My Country, 'Tis of Thee" which references "God our king."

Johnson's presentations at churches sound a lot like talks given by pseudo-historian David Barton. That's no accident since Johnson acknowledged being influenced by Barton, and the two have spoken highly of each other.[16] No one else has done more than Barton to advance the notion that church-state separation is a myth.[17] Thus, it shouldn't be surprising to see Johnson parroting Barton's arguments to try and reframe Jefferson's famous phrase as a one-way street rather than offering mutual benefit. As Johnson incorrectly put it, "The founders wanted to protect the church from an encroaching state, not the other way around."[18] That's what Barton, an evangelical and GOP activist, has been teaching politicians and pastors for

---

[14] Kaylor and Fuzy, "Christian Nationalism in the Speaker's Chair."

[15] Kaylor and Fuzy, "Christian Nationalism in the Speaker's Chair."

[16] Mike Hixenbaugh, "Meet the Evangelical Activist Who's Had a 'Profound Influence' on Speaker Mike Johnson," NBC News, October 26, 2023, https://www.nbcnews.com/news/us-news/evangelical-activist-influence-speaker-mike-johnson-rcna122313.

[17] Jack Jenkins, "The Activist Behind Opposition to the Separation of Church and State," *Religion News Service*, July 18, 2022, https://religionnews.com/2022/07/18/the-activist-behind-opposition-to-the-separation-of-church-and-state.

[18] Jack Jenkins, "Mike Johnson, Pedigreed Evangelical, Suggests His Election as House Speaker Ordained By God," *Religion News Service*, October 25, 2023, https://religionnews.com/2023/10/25/mike-johnson-a-pedigreed-evangelical-suggests-his-election-as-house-speaker-ordained-by-god.

years—even after his claims have been debunked by historians. Other politicians have piled on in more explicit ways. Rep. Lauren Boebert of Colorado argued, "I'm tired of the separation of church and state junk that's not in the Constitution. It was in a stinking letter, and it means nothing like what they say it does."[19] Doug Mastriano, a Republican state senator in Pennsylvania, denounced what he called "this myth of separation of church and state."[20] U.S. Supreme Court Justice Neil Gorsuch, during oral arguments in a case about flying the Christian flag at a city hall building, dismissed what he labeled "the so-called separation" of church and state.[21] And Ryan Walters, the Oklahoma state superintendent of public instruction, declared, "We will bring God and prayer back in schools in Oklahoma, and fight back against the radical myth of separation of church and state."[22]

Advancing the view that church-state separation doesn't exist, these politicians and others join activists like Barton and conservative preachers in pushing for Christian Nationalism. They want "In God We Trust" and the Ten Commandments hanging in public school classrooms while children are led in an official prayer. They want state funding for religious schools and houses of worship. They want Christian symbols on public property and Christian prayers inside during government meetings. They want a society where some Americans become second-class citizens because they don't adhere to the slice of conservative Christianity writing the rules.

Spoiling Democracy

Scripture cautions followers of Jesus to "beware of false prophets, who come to you in sheep's clothing but inwardly are ravenous wolves." These threats will be known "by their fruits" (Matthew 7:15–16). Given what social science has taught us about

---

[19] Jenkins, "The Activist Behind Opposition to the Separation of Church and State."

[20] Brian Kaylor and Beau Underwood, "Christian Nationalism as the Keystone," *A Public Witness*, May 12, 2022, https://publicwitness.wordandway.org/p/christian-nationalism-as-the-keystone.

[21] Brian Kaylor and Beau Underwood, "A Banner Moment for Christian Nationalism," *A Public Witness*, January 20, 2022, https://publicwitness.wordandway.org/p/a-banner-moment-for-christian-nationalism.

[22] Superintendent Ryan Walters (@RyanWaltersSupt), September 26, 2023, https://twitter.com/RyanWaltersSupt/status/1706673089692488046.

Christian Nationalism (as highlighted in chapter 2) and the stated aims of those espousing such views, there's a need to honestly assess the threat this poses to American democracy. This chapter has documented just a few egregious examples of the way Christian Nationalistic beliefs can inspire anti-democratic actions from citizens and elected leaders holding them. The specific forms may change but the fundamental issue is with a core affirmation fundamental to democratic life: that each person has an equal say in what the government does.

From wanting "In God We Trust" prominently displayed in courtrooms to having the Bible read in public classrooms, using the government as a vehicle for religious expression privileges some over others. Those wanting to carve out a special place for Christianity in the public square are implicitly (and often explicitly) okay with diminishing the status of non-Christians in society. Revisiting the arguments in chapter 3, even more vague appeals to civil religion or a "Judeo-Christian" heritage still exclude lots of people from equal participation in our common life.

Those adhering to Christian Nationalism generally root their appeals in the claim that the United States is—or at least once was—a Christian nation. It's the myth that animates the ideology. While we have not interrogated that story in detail here, others with substantial historical expertise and theological training have unpacked its misconceptions and problematic consequences.[23] Instead, we have called attention to a variety of episodes—moving flags into sanctuaries, creating congressional chaplains, adding "under God" into the Pledge, etc.—where mainline Protestants were the central actors who are now referenced by David Barton and others who push Christian Nationalism. They look to what the mainline tradition created to build support for their policy agendas and advance their visions for the country, even when the consequences erode our democratic foundations.

---

[23] Three of the best examples are: Randall Balmer, *Saving Faith: How American Christianity Can Reclaim Its Prophetic Voice* (Minneapolis: Fortress Press, 2023); Gregory Boyd, *The Myth of a Christian Nation: How the Quest for Political Power Is Destroying the Church* (Grand Rapids: Zondervan, 2007); and John Fea *Was America Founded as a Christian Nation? Revised Edition: A Historical Introduction* (Louisville: Westminster/John Knox, 2016).

The equality that undergirds democracy actually goes beyond affording everyone the same voice and vote. A more robust understanding of democratic equality involves recognizing others as political equals whose arguments and positions are not only formally entitled to a hearing but deserve our respect.[24] For democracy to flourish, the commitment has to extend beyond the process. We have to see each person as equally worthy of our consideration because of their status as a citizen engaged in the shared task of self-government. We cannot reduce someone's standing *a priori* because of their identity. All views do not warrant the same assent, but each person should receive the same deference as a stakeholder in what happens in our common life. In trying to privilege certain identities and statuses over others, Christian Nationalism seeks to create a society where all participants are not afforded equal rights by their government and equal respect from other citizens.

At the extreme, democracy serves as a means to the end of obtaining and wielding power that is quickly discarded when it no longer becomes feasible to win majority support. Christian ethicist David Gushee warns that when reactionary "Christians believe themselves to be losing significant cultural influence, facing moral or political threats to their families or institutions, and being offered the opportunity to (re)gain cultural and political power, they can prove susceptible to authoritarian, antidemocratic, Christian theocratic politics."[25] Realizing an inability to enact their preferred vision of the social order within a democratic system, this "authoritarian reactionary Christianity" tries to seize control through other means.

Such concerns are far from just hypotheticals. While seeking the GOP presidential nomination in 2016, Ben Carson—a neurosurgeon and Christian author who later became the secretary of Housing and Urban Development in the Trump administration—argued that a Muslim could not be president because the Islamic faith was

---

[24] For an extended defense of conceptualizing democracy this way, see: Robert Talisse, *Sustaining Democracy: What We Owe to the Other Side* (New York: Oxford University Press, 2021).

[25] David Gushee, *Defending Democracy from its Christian Enemies* (Grand Rapids: Eerdmans, 2023), 51.

"inconsistent with the values and principles of America."[26] While feigning loyalty to the Constitution in making this assertion, Carson ignored the constitutional protections for the free exercise of religion and prohibitions on a religious test for public office. Other politicians have similarly pushed for unconstitutional, antidemocratic efforts in a quest they frame as making America Christian again.

In 2022, two University of Maryland scholars reported alarming poll results: 70% of Americans—including 57% of Republicans—believed Christian Nationalism was unconstitutional. Specifically, they agreed the Constitution "would not allow the government to declare the U.S. a Christian nation." Yet, when asked as a follow-up question—"Do you favor or oppose the United States officially declaring the United States to be a Christian nation?"—the researchers found that "61% of Republicans supported declaring the United States a Christian nation." Despite more than half of GOP respondents acknowledging such a statement to be unconstitutional, a majority favored making it anyway.[27]

To cite a third example, *CBS News* profiled a pastor named Ken Peters involved in leading a church network where Christian Nationalism is fervently proclaimed. Propagating a narrative of moral and national decline, Peters perceived his efforts to be a bulwark against cultural erosion and described himself as fighting so hard to "keep [the United States] a Christian nation." He sought a country structured according to "Christian principles and Christian laws and Christian ways."[28] (It's worth mentioning that Brian's ministry advocating for the protection of church-state separation was also featured in the same film as a contrast to those, like Peters, pushing for Christian Nationalism.)

[26] Eric Bradner, "Ben Carson: U.S. Shouldn't Elect a Muslim President," CNN, September 21, 2015, https://www.cnn.com/2015/09/20/politics/ben-carson-muslim-president-2016/index.html.

[27] Stella Rouse and Shibley Telhami, "Most Republicans Support Declaring the United States a Christian Nation," *Politico*, September 21, 2022, https://www.politico.com/news/magazine/2022/09/21/most-republicans-support-declaring-the-united-states-a-christian-nation-00057736.

[28] Taylor Mooney, "Is America a Christian Nation? Pastors at Odds about Fusion of Faith and Politics," *CBS News*, March 4, 2021, https://www.cbsnews.com/news/america-christian-nation-religious-right.

Similar stories could be told around gerrymanders and voting restrictions, about conspiracy theories and unsubstantiated claims of election fraud. From wanting to change the rules to not respecting the outcomes of the democratic process, the authoritarian streak running through parts of American Christianity with the goal of reclaiming what has been mythically lost through demographic and cultural change shows little interest in protecting democratic norms and institutions.

Christian Nationalism is not democracy's friend, but there are resources within the Christian tradition that can aid democracy's cause. For instance, Gushee roots his support of democracy in the traditions of two particular groups: Baptists and Black Christians.[29] The former saw state authoritarianism as a threat to God-given conscience, thus it developed a robust understanding of religious liberty. The latter saw how the evil of state power could be used to deny the God-given equality inherent among human beings. Democracy provides the political space for these principles to be expressed and protected.

The enormity of preserving and bolstering democracy can make any one person or group feel overwhelmed. Where does one start? How can one person have an impact? Seeking practical answers, political scientist Christopher Beem turns to the cultivation and practice of virtues as a healing balm. By intentionally attending to individual citizens entering into democratic debate and decision-making, we can mold ourselves into better participants by drawing on the wisdom of the cardinal and theological virtues to recast them in service to sustaining democracy. Beem argued in his book *The Seven Democratic Virtues*:

> Virtue represents a social agreement. A society agrees and affirms that certain habits and behaviors are important, valuable, and help us understand who we are. ... Even in the midst of our nation's greatest challenges, there have been *enough* citizens who did agree, who did strive to live up to the virtues that were most important for the times in which they found themselves. There is no reason to assume

---

[29] See chapters 12 and 13 of Gushee, *Defending Democracy from Its Christian Enemies.*

that this moment of crisis is somehow unlike all those that came before.[30]

In other words, this is a time for citizens to recommit themselves to the democratic tradition. There's a need to relearn what it requires and teach those commitments. Rather than locating our primary political identities within a particular party, it's imperative that we give our loyalty to democracy itself.

That raises another thorny issue for Christians. Democracy makes no assertions about what is ultimately good. Instead, it protects the freedom of individuals and collectives to pursue their own interests and live in accordance with their particular values, provided they do not try to impede others from doing the same. Political theorists have long noted this system can be an odd fit for religious adherents whose faith convictions perceive such freedom as an affront to the will of God—a will that they are confident they grasp and equally certain their opponents do not. Indeed, one way of understanding Christian Nationalism is that the freedom democracy affords has been used to create a society that its purveyors believe neglects God's blessing and desires. Thus, the authoritarian turn is justified to correct these abuses democracy allows and return the United States to their understanding of the righteous path.

Such logic demonstrates why Christians need to not only challenge the theological missteps of Christian Nationalism but also offer a robust defense of democracy itself. In *Politics as a Christian Vocation*, Franklin Gamwell did exactly that. During both biblical times and throughout much of history, Christians (and others) had little influence over what the state did. The emergence of democracy radically changed that. Gamwell's book argues that in democratic societies, "citizens generally have a real opportunity to help shape the political order." From this it follows that "given the profound consequences of political rule for worldly good and evil, circumstances now imply that active resistance to political wrongs and deliberate pursuit of justice belong to the vocations of Christians generally because they are called to help 'everyone, wherever possible' or to love their neighbors as themselves."[31]

The ideology of Christian Nationalism promotes a social order—legitimized with Christian language and ideas—where the rights and flourishing of some are privileged at the expense of others. Seeking to achieve its goals through whatever means are achievable, it turns on democracy when majority rule no longer serves its purposes. The need is urgent for Christians to rally to democracy's defense to prevent future erosion of its principles and norms in American society. In doing so, not only can we exercise the power democracy grants to each citizen, but we can also fulfill the greatest commandment Jesus teaches us. To protect democracy so all can flourish is a key way we love our neighbors as ourselves in public life.

---

[31] Franklin Gamwell, *Politics as a Christian Vocation: Faith and Democracy Today*, (Chicago: University of Chicago Press, 2005), 25.

Chapter 11

FAILED CHURCH

St. George's United Methodist Church in Philadelphia is a historic house of worship. Not only is it the oldest Methodist church in continuous use in the United States, but it's also seen quite a few significant moments since its founding in 1767. The first Methodist hymnal was published there, and the Methodist statement of faith was presented to Americans for the first time at the church. Rev. Francis Asbury, one of the first two bishops of the Methodist Episcopal Church, preached his first American sermon there and called it "the cathedral church of American Methodism."[1] The church licensed the first two African American Methodist preachers, Rev. Richard Allen and Rev. Absalom Jones. Three years later, most of the Black members of the congregation left with Allen in protest of racial segregation during worship, thus leading to the formation of the African Methodist Episcopal denomination.

Today, the congregation leans into its progressive, inclusive nature. The congregation has spent decades working on reckoning with its past racism, and it bills itself as "a reconciling and LGBTQ+ affirming United Methodist church." As the nation's largest mainline Protestant denomination split in 2019-2023 over the issue of homosexuality, St. George's stayed with the denomination in favor of inclusion and affirmation. Yet, like many progressive mainline Protestant denominations that would generally find themselves on the opposite side of most issues embraced by the pro-Trump mob that ransacked the U.S. Capitol on January 6, 2021, there are times

---

[1] "Our Story," Historic St. George's United Methodist Church, https://www.historicstgeorges.org/story.

when Christian Nationalism—similar to other bad theological habits that are hard to break—still works its way into worship.

For instance, the St. George's service on July 2, 2023—the Sunday closest to the Fourth of July that year—started with a nationalistic call to worship. Although drawn from biblical passages like Psalm 33 and Deuteronomy 8, declaring such words without context after noting it was the Fourth of July weekend colored the interpretation.

"Blessed is the country with God, for God," the pastor declared. "Make the country strong. ... Bless God your God for all the good land he has given you."[2]

After a service full of hymns, prayers, and a sermon without nationalistic references, the congregation partook of communion, prayed, and sang a closing song: "My Country, 'Tis of Thee." Bookending the service as part of the holy worship, the blessing and patriotic song from the hymnal sacralized the Fourth of July as a holy occasion and taught parishioners to view their nation through a Christian Nationalistic lens.

St. George's UMC is hardly unique in its worship. Such soft Christian Nationalism can be found in the hymns, prayers, liturgical responses, and sermons in mainline congregations across the country, especially on Sundays close to non-liturgical, patriotic holidays like Memorial Day, Veterans Day, and especially the Fourth of July. Even as the mainline tradition's sway over American culture has dramatically lessened, it remains difficult to disentangle these nationalistic influences from the worship offered in their churches.

It might be tempting to overlook this version as harmless, but as we've shown throughout this book, such moments are holdovers from more substantive efforts at mixing the sacred and the secular. And such moments, worked seamlessly into worship, continue to disciple congregants in the way of Christian Nationalism. Empowering this heretical ideology has also helped lead to more extreme expressions. Decades of mainline Protestants practicing Christian Nationalism helped move the ideology into the mainstream of Christian churches and movements. And as the January 6 insurrection demonstrated,

---

[2] Facebook page of St. George's United Methodist Church, July 2, 2023, https://www.facebook.com/historicstgeorges/ videos/597620022501470.

it can be particularly dangerous and heretical when mixed with extremist politics. To show how Christian Nationalism is leading people away from the gospel, we'll take you inside one of the worst worship services we've seen. This is the world mainline Protestants helped create and that some far-right evangelicals and Pentecostals now lead.

The Church of MAGA

"I've got a prophetic word for you: We win. We win! I've got a word for you, Church, the Church of the Lord Jesus. I've got a word for you, body of Christ: we win."[3]

With those words, Marty Grisham christened the ReAwaken America Tour event in Branson, Missouri, in November 2022 as the Church and body of Christ. The head of a Pentecostal ministry called "Loudmouth prayer," Grisham offered this promise of victory while sharing the stage with MAGA political figures including Eric Trump, Michael Flynn, Kash Patel, pillow-hugger Mike Lindell, and people who participated in the January 6, 2021, insurrection. Yet, Grisham wasn't alone in framing the two-day rally as a gathering of the body of Christ. Anna Khait, a former contestant on the TV reality show *Survivor*, called those gathered at the ReAwaken event "the light," thus invoking a metaphor Jesus used about those following him.

"This country is in darkness. We are the light in the darkness," she said. "And it's only by the grace of God, amen."

Similarly, "prophet" Julie Green described those at the event in religious terms traditionally used to refer to God's people. She made the declaration after prophesying in the name of God that former President Donald Trump would soon return to the Oval Office.

"How many [are] excited that our president, Trump, is coming back?" she asked to loud cheers. "They can't intimidate this body of Christ because we are something different. We are the remnant, and we will not back off, we will not back down, and because we know that God is on our side and we win."

---

[3] Brian Kaylor, "The ReAwaken America Worship Service in Branson," *A Public Witness*, November 8, 2022, https://publicwitness.wordandway.org/p/the-reawaken-america-worship-service.

Such rhetoric might seem odd at a political rally, but it accurately describes the way they acted. This traveling variety show of Christian Nationalism, anti-vaccine rhetoric, QAnon conspiracies, and election denialism is more than just another political event. It includes times of congregational singing of praise music, prayers, sermons, and even baptisms. This MAGA revival that's been going around the nation since 2021 cannot be fully understood in merely partisan terms.

The ReAwaken America Tour (or RAT for short) has gone through multiple iterations. We experienced it firsthand when it came to Branson, covering what occurs so that you don't have to watch (you're welcome). Seeing it up close made clear how much the political event drew on liturgical and religious elements, and it's obvious they saw this as a church gathering. So we'll share the highlights (or perhaps more accurately, the lowlights) of the event by considering it in the form of a church service. It's okay if you don't have a bulletin, we'll walk you through it.

Call to worship.

The service in Branson started like other ReAwaken America events. "Prophet" Amanda Grace led a group of people in blowing shofars seven times to kick off each day of the event. Journalist Sarah Posner, author of *Unholy*, previously documented the co-option of this Jewish instrument at Christian Nationalistic events (including during the January 6 insurrection).[4] Grace also predicted the 2022 midterm elections would be part of bringing Trump back to the White House since it would happen on a "blood moon" day. Preacher Dave Scarlett explained why they would be blowing the shofars:

> That's what we're here for: to get America back to our King of kings and Lord of hosts. So to bring in the spiritual realm, we always ask the Father to come, the Son to come, and we're going to invite the Holy Spirit to come. And how we do that, we blow into the shofar. We're ready to go to war with the enemy in the spiritual realm and the physical realm to take our country back in the name of Jesus Christ.

---

[4] Sarah Posner, "Look Who's Blowing Shofars," *Moment*, March 25, 2022, https://momentmag.com/opinion-shofars-christian-nationalism.

Songs of praise.

Before speakers came up to talk about how the COVID-19 pandemic was a fraud, vaccines were dangerous, the 2020 election was stolen, and 5G networks were a plot of the new world order, both days started with congregational songs led by the worship team from Influence Church in Anaheim, California. The chosen songs for this service included "How Great is Our God," "Our God Reigns," "Lion and the Lamb," "Goodness of God," and "Shout to the Lord."

Greeting.

Since this service was devoted to praising, defending, and prophesying the return of Donald Trump, it's critical to have an official priest of the church to bring formal greetings. Eric Trump has often filled that role (and sometimes Donald Jr.; Eric's wife, Lara; or Junior's fiancé, Kimberly Guilfoyle). On a few occasions, Eric has even called his dad during a ReAwaken event and held the phone up to the microphone for the former president to greet his fans. In Branson, Eric walked onto the stage as a video montage of his dad dancing played on the big screens.

"Guys, we love you. You guys are so incredible. And it is good to be here," Eric said. "And you see all these American flags. Right, this is real America."

He praised the "MAGA" crowd as "people who love God, they love the American flag, they love the Pledge of Allegiance." And before the official 2024 announcement, he insisted his father would run for president again to fight for Christianity.

"Now you look at this country, and you know how hard this is for me? You know, we were out there every single day fighting and fighting and fighting against all odds. Actually, we had the best odd of all, which was the guy up there," Eric said as he pointed upward and recounted his father's presidency with "we" language. "We will never ever ever stop fighting. This family will never ever ever stop fighting."

The congregation then stood and chanted, "We love Trump! We love Trump! We love Trump!"

Prayer.

Jackson Lahmeyer, an Oklahoma pastor and failed U.S. Senate candidate who proudly embraces the term "Christian Nationalist,"[5] led the congregation in a prayer after he preached. He asked everyone to stand and hold up their hands so they could experience the Holy Spirit to receive "a holy boldness" necessary to continue the work.

"Father, it is my request that right now fresh fire would fall in this place," he prayed. "We receive the Holy Spirit, a fresh infilling so that we can leave this place with power, with power, with divine power."

Responsive reading.

Clay Clark, the organizer and emcee of the ReAwaken America Tour,[6] likes to lead a litany at the events. The people, many of whom trek to various ReAwaken services as it moves around the nation, enthusiastically join in.

> Clark: "How many of you believe that Jesus is King?"
> People: "Yeah!"
> Clark: "How many of you believe that President Donald J. Trump is, in fact, our president?"
> People: "Yeah!"
> Clark: "And how many of you believe that General Flynn is America's general?"
> People: "Yeah!"

Offering.

While many churches dropped the offertory time during the COVID pandemic, ReAwaken continues to push the giving times. Perhaps that's not surprising since they preach that the pandemic was fake, but it's also because this is a profit-ic enterprise. Nearly every speaker has something to sell, many of them putting their

[5] Brian Kaylor and Beau Underwood, "How Most Christians Became Godless Globalists," *A Public Witness*, October 25, 2022, https://publicwitness.wordandway.org/p/how-most-christians-became-godless.

[6] For an excellent profile of Clark, see: Sam Kestenbaum, "'I Think All the Christians Get Slaughtered': Inside the MAGA Road Show Barnstorming America," *Rolling Stone*, September 17, 2022, https://www.rollingstone.com/culture/culture-features/clay-clark-reawaken-america-maga-tour-trump-1234594574.

websites or QR codes on the screen during their presentation—with Clay Clark often coming on stage to reiterate how people can learn more, buy things, or donate. Clark and Michael Flynn even urge the congregants to invest in gold and silver.

The tithing doesn't have to be just online. Dozens of vendors—including booths for many of the speakers—were just steps away from the auditorium. The Trump store sat just outside the doors, with others a bit farther away under a big revival tent outside. There one could buy "Fight Like a Flynn" shirts, Clark's books, beauty products to make you look "5-10 years younger," golden Trump coins from a "prophet," lots of products praising Jesus and/or cursing Biden, crystal power pendants, products to protect you from COVID or vaccines, artwork showing Trump and Flynn as Revolutionary heroes, some sort of fabric to "protect" you from 5G radiation, and towels from MyPillow (which we don't think are supposed to be used as pillows).

Baptism.

This religious movement is bringing converts into its fold—literally. During a baptism service in the swimming pool of a nearby hotel, around 150 ReAwaken attendees lined up to be baptized. With many wearing their pro-Trump, anti-Biden, or Americana clothing, they took turns being plunged beneath the chlorinated water. Several couples were both baptized, as were children and multiple generations of some families—all while a band nearby sang Christian music. Organizers say nearly 5,000 people were baptized during the first 17 ReAwaken events.

Scripture reading.

"Prophet" Julie Green came forward to offer a word from the Lord. But rather than open a Bible app, she first read some of her previous "prophecies" on her phone before sensing God had a fresh one for her to deliver (which conveniently coincided with her speaking timeslot). Earlier in 2022, Green campaigned for Doug Mastriano in his run for governor of Pennsylvania, when she had prophesied, "'Doug Mastriano, I have you here for such a time as this,' saith the Lord."[7] But a few days after the RAT event in Branson, Mastriano lost in a landslide. Like she did with Mastriano, she borrowed biblical phrases in her new "prophecy" about how Trump—whom she has repeatedly called a new "David"—was coming back into office soon:

> For I the Lord this day am telling my children to receive your victory as I have shown you in my words and through my prophets that I speak to them and I give them what's going to happen before it happens. My country, my nation of the United States of America, receive your victory this day because as your elections draw near, do not be afraid of the fraud because I am bringing that fraud down. That fraud is not bigger than me.

With her eyes closed and still speaking as if for God, she added:

> I told you before that I am cleansing your House, that I am cleansing your Senate, and, yes, I am cleansing the White House. Those people who are there, those people who have stolen your nation, I am bringing them all down. ... So to my children and to my body, I am telling you this day that I am bringing this victory. I am getting you your nation back. You are winning these elections. You are getting my David. My David is my son, and no one will stop him from taking his place, his rightful place of power. What has been stolen will be given back.

Special music.

Simone Gold, a physician known for opposing COVID-19 vaccines and being arrested for her role during the Capitol insurrection, received the rock star treatment at ReAwaken less than two months after being released from prison for her January 6 activity. For her entrance, the service included "We Are the Champions" by Queen as photos of Gold appeared on the big screens.

"I've done my sentence but committed no crime," the music declared along with photos of Gold in the Capitol on January 6.

---

[7] Brian Kaylor and Beau Underwood, "Christian Nationalism as the Keystone," *A Public Witness*, May 12, 2022, https://publicwitness. wordandway.org/p/christian-nationalism-as-the-keystone.

"But it's been no bed of roses, no pleasure cruise," the song continued as the screens played clips of media outlets that "canceled" Gold and stock prison footage before Gold walked out during the chorus to rapturous applause.

Sermon.

Lance Wallnau, a "prophet" who had been stumping for GOP candidates for that year's midterm elections, offered the main sermon at ReAwaken in Branson. Wallnau, who has embraced the term "Christian Nationalist," is perhaps best known for popularizing the claim that Trump was like King Cyrus, which Wallnau came to by reading Isaiah 45 since Trump was the 45th president. That seemed like a bizarre idea until he started talking in Branson.

Wallnau walked the congregation through a couple of texts. First, he invoked the parable of the sheep and the goats in Matthew 25 as he urged people not to be afraid of being called a "Christian Nationalist." As he explained, he sees the sheep not as those helping the least of these (since apparently only a Marxist would say that) but as those protecting national sovereignty. He declared:

> What's coming down in the last days—and all the theologians fight me on it, but so what. When Jesus comes back, the Bible says he's going to gather all the nations in front of him and separate them into sheep and goat categories. Understand something, the sheep nations, by instinct what you're doing is preserving the sovereignty of the United States from being broken down and assimilated as a beat-up junior partner in a global empire. We will always be separate from that system.

Wallnau then jumped to Luke 2:34 to offer a "prophecy." In that verse, Simeon makes a prophecy about the baby Jesus being one that will "be spoken against." To connect the dots from Jesus to ReAwaken, Wallnau interjected, "This movement is in its infancy, but it's about to grow very quickly." And, Wallnau added, they are being spoken against, a framing that puts the movement in the place of Jesus in the words from Simeon. Wallnau then noted that on the Jewish calendar this is the year 5783, which he decided offered another clue.

"If you go to Strong's Concordance, there's a word in Greek and a word in Hebrew next to all these different words," Wallanu said.

"What word in the Concordance actually corresponds with 5783? And it means to expose that and make it naked, to reveal what has been hidden."

The congregation cheered and many nodded their heads in agreement.

"This is our year to see the exposure, and you're starting to see it already happen. You don't think that God had his hand in putting Elon Musk over Twitter?" Wallnau added. "Elon is doing a splendid job of opening up and exposing things right now. This election is going to be the exposure of things right now. And the spirit of the Lord says it's a sign that will be spoken against."

To recap in case you got lost, we can take a prophecy about baby Jesus and a word used in Habakkuk to predict things like a billionaire buying a social media app thousands of years later because this is a young movement and there's a word that happens to be the 5,783rd word in a book listing biblical words. (Warning: don't try that kind of exegesis in a seminary paper.)

Altar call.

During both days of ReAwaken, people were invited to come forward for prayer and to have a "prophet" like Amanda Grace or Julie Green put hands on them. Both days the aisles and hallways filled with long lines, with some people seeking a prayer of healing. Many people fell to the ground after being touched.

Song of response.

As the service neared its close, Christian musician Sean Feucht went on stage to lead a round of worship. As he noted between songs, he had recently performed during campaign rallies for Arizona gubernatorial hopeful Kari Lake and Pennsylvania gubernatorial hopeful Doug Mastriano (and he had said they would both win but neither did).

At Branson, he urged people to join him in "a prophetic moment" for MAGA victories in the midterm elections. He recounted the story from 2 Kings 13 in which the prophet Elisha told Israel's king to strike the ground with a handful of arrows, but since the king did it only three times he received a limited victory. Feucht then told everyone to hold up an imaginary arrow in their hands and strike the ground much more than three times to bring victory in the midterms. So the congregation shouted "strike" a couple dozen times while chopping the air to the beats of the music before giving a large shout together.

Benediction.

Michael Flynn, the main face of ReAwaken, came to the stage to close out the service. He thanked everyone for coming. He gave them a call to live out what they had learned by voting and getting involved more locally to help the movement grow. Flynn, who during a previous ReAwaken event urged pastors to preach about the Constitution more than the Bible[8] and talked about the importance of being "one nation under God,"[9] also offered a Christian Nationalistic blessing at the end of the Branson event:

> The Judeo-Christian values that this country was created upon, very serious thing to me. Our Constitution is a, it's a fulfillment of a promise that we make to each other as Americans, just as the Bible is a fulfillment of the promises that we make to each other as Christians on this planet. And anybody that believes—anybody that believes—the Bible is a very powerful thing, as is the Constitution. And those promises are things like the Bill of Rights, things like the Ten Commandments.

Converting Christians to "Nones"

You might be tempted to dismiss the ReAwaken America Tour and the religious carnival barkers who speak at it as fringe and extreme. While that is certainly true, ignoring their influence is a mistake. There are increasingly louder alarms about the damage this type of politicized religion is inflicting on American churches. One of the sad ironies of Christian Nationalism is that its misguided quest to portray the United States as a Christian nation is fueling an exodus

---

[8] Brian Kaylor and Beau Underwood, "The Sermon Michael Flynn Hopes You'll Hear," *A Public Witness*, July 14, 2022, https://publicwitness.wordandway.org/p/the-sermon-michael-flynn-hopes-youll.

[9] Brian Kaylor and Beau Underwood, "One Nation Under Michael Flynn's God?" *A Public Witness*, November 16, 2021, https://publicwitness.wordandway.org/p/one-nation-under-michael-flynns-god.

from Christian communities. Our society is becoming more secular partially because of the professed Christians shouting the loudest.

Recent survey data on religious identification revealed something quite odd: more people are claiming the label "evangelical" despite not attending church services.[10] An increasing number of respondents call themselves evangelicals despite belonging to a non-Christian faith tradition. It's a strange use of a category that historically has held strong religious connotations. Political scientist and American Baptist pastor Ryan Burge argued:

> What it means to be evangelical is being radically remade. It used to be that when many people thought about evangelicalism, they conjured up an image of a fiery preacher imploring them to accept Jesus. Now the data indicate that more and more Americans are conflating evangelicalism with Republicanism—and melding two forces to create a movement that is not entirely about politics or religion but power.[11]

It stands to reason that to the extent our culture equates religious belonging with partisan identity, those who reject one label will also refuse the other. If being Christian is associated with a single political party or support for a specific candidate—especially when wrapped up in the trappings of an event like RAT—then those who vote a different way or vigorously dislike a particular politician may also jettison their religious affiliation as part of repudiating the politics connected to it. When faith is reduced to a partisan platform, belonging to one means identifying with the other and vice versa.

Recognizing this should cause great pause to those concerned about the rise of the "Nones." A growing number of Americans no longer formally identify with a religious tradition. This trend, which is more pronounced amongst younger generations, means pews are emptying. It is sapping congregations of the resources needed

---

[10] Kate Shellnut, "'Political Evangelicals'? More Trump Supporters Adopt the Label," *Christianity Today*, September 16, 2021, https://www.christianitytoday.com/news/2021/september/trump-evangelical-identity-pew-research-survey-presidency.html.

[11] Ryan Burge, "Why 'Evangelical' is Becoming Another Word for 'Republican,'" *New York Times*, October 26, 2021, https://www.nytimes.com/2021/10/26/opinion/evangelical-republican.html.

for mission. More and more churches are closing, while others are struggling to even maintain their existence. The vitality of American Christianity appears to be on the wane.

This is a complicated phenomenon. But Burge, a leading expert on the topic and author of *The Nones: Where They Came From, Who They Are, and Where They Are Going*, looked at the data on religious disaffiliation and noted a correlation with the politicization of faith. Thus, he tentatively concluded, "It doesn't take a huge causal leap to believe that as the loudest and most numerous voices in Protestant Christianity became more theologically and politically conservative, that drove off a lot of moderates."[12] Logic would hold that as this trend continued, with Christianity becoming intertwined with far-fetched political conspiracies and extremist thinking, many people exit churches to make a statement about both their religious and their political beliefs.[13]

Research conducted by another social scientist, Stephen Bullivant, corroborates this idea. Interviewing "nonverts" (those who previously claimed a religious affiliation but no longer do) across the United States, he provided qualitative detail to help understand the macro shifts indicated in the quantitative surveys. Introducing one interview comment, Bullivant described a couple participating in his study as perceiving the evangelical Christian world they left behind as "stuck in a toxically codependent relationship with the GOP." Specifically, they asserted:

> Republicanism *is* the religion, and they've been fighting for that for at least 25 years—just to turn it into a religion. So that it doesn't matter what they do—and let's be honest, Trump is probably one of the worst humans in the whole universe—my dad will never be able to do anything other than be on this "religion team" because he's told that it's *his* religion team. And all they have to do is play their religion card and it's like, "Religion team says this," and he gets to

---

[12] Ryan Burge, *The Nones: Where They Came From, Who They Are, and Where They Are Going* (Minneapolis: Fortress, 2023), 70.

[13] Other scholars are in agreement with Burge's explanation. For an overview of the research, see Amelia Thomson-DeVeauz and Daniel Cox, "The Christian Right Is Helping Drive Liberals Away From Religion," *FiveThirtyEight*, September 18, 2019, https://fivethirtyeight.com/features/the-christian-right-is-helping-drive-liberals-away-from-religion.

turn his whole brain off and do everything against what he says.[14]

Reducing religion to political tribalism makes Christian faith appear unprincipled and hypocritical. The attractiveness of its ideas and values becomes overshadowed by its misuse and abuse for partisan ends. Maybe too many people are throwing the baby out with the proverbial bathwater, but clearly a lot of people no longer believe Christian faith is redeemable from the way it's been used to commit political sins. To use the language of marketing, Christian Nationalism is bad branding that soils the entire American Church. While mainline Protestants helped lay the foundation for the larger edifice, the worst offenses now emanate from other corners, but they still sully everyone's reputation. Unlike the business world, this is not a problem that can be solved by a logo refresh or a clever name change. To the extent that non-Christians equate following Jesus with strident politics and fringe viewpoints, it becomes more difficult for the gospel to gain a fresh hearing.

There's no easy way to overcome all this guilt by association. But the path forward involves clearer distinctions between the claims and mission of the church vis-a-vis national identity and political agendas. We first need to be able to say that *this* not *that*. We must help people see that Christian Nationalism is not Christianity, whether it's found in a far-right rally or a progressive Fourth of July service.

[14] Stephen Bullivant, *Nonverts: The Making of Ex-Christian America* (New York: Oxford, 2022), 147.

Chapter 12

MOVING FORWARD

"Get to know them, spend some time with them," is the advice Episcopal Presiding Bishop Michael Curry has offered for engaging those with Christian Nationalistic views. He understandably believes that conversion is possible through building relationships and trust. But his goal is to "counter these negative perversions of Christianity and of our humanity ... with an affirmative positive way of being Christian."[1]

John Dorhauer, the former general minister and president of the United Church of Christ, has seemed less enthusiastic about such an approach. He said during a 2022 online forum:

I seek to engage progressive Christianity in a deep conversation about just what is needed to send these bigots and homophobes and misogynists back under the rocks out from which they crawled when the 45th president took office and brought their brand of Christian Nationalism back to the center and put them back in power. ... The complacency and the decorum characteristic of White Christian liberalism is not going to bring back the justice we seek, nor mitigate the damage being done by those whose brand of Christianity calls them to engage in holy war."[2]

---

[1] Mya Jaradat, "How Americans Can Address Christian Nationalism in Their Congregations and Communities," *Deseret News*, February 8, 2021, https://www.deseret.com/indepth/2021/2/7/22254802/how-to-address-christian-nationalism-extreme-militant-white-pastors-citizens-deradicalize-democracy.

[2] Maic D'Agostino, "'Don't be Silent About This': UCC General Minister Takes on Christian Nationalism," United Church of Christ, November 10, 2022, https://www.ucc.org/dont-be-silent-about-this-ucc-general-minister-takes-on-christian-nationalism.

While Dorhauer sought defeat and banishment in contrast to Curry's suggestion of engagement and persuasion, both mainline leaders see Christian Nationalism as a problem of "the other." Those holding these beliefs are outsiders who can be reached only by crossing boundaries. They may disagree over what that boundary crossing should look like but both depict this dynamic in us-versus-them language.

By now, we hope the arguments of this book have convinced you otherwise. In a variety of ways, these denominations inadvertently fueled its rise. While many mainline Protestants condemn the Christian Nationalism of conservative evangelicals and Pentecostals, much of this ideology emerged from closer to home. It's a religious version of *Frankenstein*.

In the Sermon on the Mount, Jesus warned his followers against judgments unless they were willing to be held to the same standards they employ. He called out those pointing to faults in others when they themselves suffered even more severely from the same imperfections: "Why do you see the speck in your neighbor's eye but do not notice the log in your own eye? Or how can you say to your neighbor, 'Let me take the speck out of your eye,' while the log is in your own eye? You hypocrite, first take the log out of your own eye, and then you will see clearly to take the speck out of your neighbor's eye" (Matthew 7:3-5). It's time to apply Jesus's logic to Christian Nationalism. Mainline and more progressive Christians need to stop seeing this issue as solely the problem of others. There's an urgent need to interrogate logs in the eyes of our own groups rather than merely pointing out the specks (or even large logs) in the eyes of others.

Some will protest that this is a waste of time because the larger problem exists within more conservative denominations and churches, especially those on the fringe of American Christianity. They will argue that the most urgent challenge is calling out these bad actors and the way they abuse the name "Christian" for partisan purposes that seek to protect a social order that privileges straight, White men. Bluntly, we disagree. This answer takes the easy way out, involving the condemnation of others and requiring change on their part without any introspection and adjustments from oneself. Challenging egregious representations of Christianity is important—and we do that often at *Word&Way*'s award-winning Substack newsletter, *A Public Witness*. But that doesn't mean we should ignore areas most likely to be fruitful for progress within our own churches, denominations, and organizations.

Additionally, it's important to note that mainline Protestant embrace of Christian Nationalism isn't just a problem in the past. We've focused on the story of how mainliners helped create Christian Nationalism. But it's also still in the pews and even pulpits. Consider some of the findings from PRRI in 2023. While they found White evangelicals to be the religious group most embracing of Christian Nationalism with 64% categorized as adherents or sympathizers, one-third of White mainline Protestants also matched that profile.[3] Even on an issue like support for political violence—which research shows is something adherents of Christian Nationalism often support—mainline Protestants aren't doing much better than evangelicals. PRRI in 2023 found that 31% of White evangelicals agreed that "because things have gotten so far off track, true American patriots may have to resort to violence in order to save our country." That made evangelicals the religious group most likely to agree with needing political violence. But White mainline Protestants were second at 25%.[4] All of this isn't just a problem with churchgoers not listening to their clergy. Many mainline ministers in 2023 still adhere to key Christian Nationalistic ideals. For instance, 12% of mainline clergy agree that "God intended America to be a new promised land where European Christians could create a society that could be an example to the rest of the world," and 51% disagree that "the U.S. would benefit from having more elected leaders who follow religions other than Christianity or who are not religious at all."[5]

---

[3] "A Christian Nation? Understanding the Threat of Christian Nationalism to American Democracy and Culture," PRRI, February 8, 2023, https://www.prri.org/research/a-christian-nation-understanding-the-threat-of-christian-nationalism-to-american-democracy-and-culture.

[4] "Threats to American Democracy Ahead of an Unprecedented Presidential Election," PRRI, October 25, 2023, https://www.prri.org/research/threats-to-american-democracy-ahead-of-an-unprecedented-presidential-election.

[5] "Clergy and Congregations in a Time of Transformation: Findings from the 2022–2023 Mainline Protestant Clergy Survey," PRRI, September 13, 2023, https://www.prri.org/research/clergy-and-congregations-in-a-time-of-transformation-findings-from-the-2022-2023-mainline-protestant-clergy-survey.

Clearly, it takes time—and deliberate actions—to detox. So getting our own houses in order could make a difference in the body politic.

Taking Action to Combat Christian Nationalism

With regard to Christian Nationalism, a lot of progress can be made by focusing on ourselves. Mainline and progressive Christian communities can examine their own words and practices to reduce or eliminate expressions of Christian Nationalism. Within both church and society, action follows awareness. Progressively-minded Christians (and others) are quite adept at pointing out the specks (and logs) in the eyes of those on the political and theological right when it comes to expressions of Christian Nationalism. Yet, this threat to American public life and the Church's public witness will not be eliminated until mainline Protestants remove the logs in their own eyes as well. By doing so, they reduce the influence of the ideology in our society. Moreover, they create an alternative witness whose stark contrast with Christian Nationalism helps other followers of Jesus sort out the wheat from the chaff. Addressing Christian Nationalism in our own congregations is an opportunity for discipleship.

Consider the example of Olin T. Binkley Memorial Baptist Church in Chapel Hill, North Carolina. When the American Baptist congregation sought to document its congregational history, it was proud of its progressive track record on civil rights, LGBTQ inclusion, and social justice activism. Yet, as the church imagined its future, it wanted an honest accounting of its past. So it solicited a scholar to put together a new and comprehensive history of the church without glossing over the blemishes of the years gone by. Jeff Brumley of *Baptist News Global* described the ambitious project as including "the conflict around the construction of the church sanctuary, the licensing of a gay Duke Divinity School student, and a debate over ordaining a Black seminarian who opposed same-sex relationships. Disagreements over these and other issues often led to hurt feelings and even the loss of members." He added that the congregation continues to tackle difficult issues, including Christian Nationalism and "the ways the congregation has contributed to those ideologies."

"So many of our book studies have looked at how does a White, progressive church like Binkley, with a high concentration of learned folk, look in the mirror a little differently to acknowledge our own culpability and complicity in the systems that make it such that African Americans and others are oppressed," Binkley's senior pastor, Marcus McFaul, explained.[6]

If Christians really believe that truth sets us free, then such reckonings like the one undertaken at Binkley Memorial are more gift than threat. In improving the accuracy of how we tell our own stories, they allow us to celebrate the ways our witness has built up the body of Christ and to practice repentance in those places where we have fallen short of the glory of God. Mainline leaders, denominations, and churches wanting to address Christian Nationalism can start by looking in the mirror. They can acknowledge and remedy their own contributions to the spread of this ideology. Here are a few suggestions on how that work might be done:

1. Learn Your Congregation's Story. Churches are fascinating organizations. Many mainline congregations have long, rich histories. They often have played (and still do play) influential roles in their communities. There's a particular culture within each church: a logic to why things happen in the ways they do, stories that are remembered and others deemphasized, and certain values and practices held more tightly than others. In this era of diminished denominational loyalty, many members may not know much about their specific tradition or the history of the congregation. Their newness comes with an unawareness of the congregation's past events and present culture, for better and for worse.

Attending to these details by intentionally investigating and discussing a church's own story can be a rich way of exploring Christian Nationalism in a local context. When has the church offered its support to the state, and when has it stood in critique? If the church observes patriotic holidays or holds national symbols in reverence, when did that start and why? Every church has a story that involves primary and secondary actors, tensions and conflicts, poignant episodes, and moments of resolution. By exploring the stories in the church's past, members can better understand themselves in the present. History illuminates both how the current

---

[6] Jeff Brumley, "This Church Wanted an Examination of Its History, Not Just a Coffee Table Book," *Baptist News Global*, July 18, 2023, https://baptistnews.com/article/this-church-wanted-an-examination-of-its-history-not-just-a-coffee-table-book.

expression of a church came to be and inflection points that allow a congregation to imagine what might have been had a different path been chosen.

Moreover, a church's story can serve as a guide into its future.[7] Making the story explicit allows a faith community to foster a sense of identity and common witness. Such a practice can cultivate new directions and hopes that maintain continuity where desired and chart new paths where needed. Above all, it offers an important reminder that the journey is undertaken among a group committed to a life together and that God is also present in the unfolding drama of that people and place.

In regard to Christian Nationalism, rich conversations around the congregation's story allow a community to say "this is where we have been on this issue" and "this is how we want to be going forward." Those two statements may be similar, or they might reflect a dramatic shift. Focusing on a church's story also reorients the debate. The conversation is not about individual political views or rival factions. Instead, it's about the values a community wants to embody in its worship and mission, along with goals it wants to realize together and the concrete steps it will take to realize them. The way forward becomes about writing the next chapter of the story together.

2. Educate Your Church and Community. While awareness of Christian Nationalism and its dangers is growing, the phenomenon is still poorly understood. Many hear the phrase and confuse the ideology with patriotism itself. Others struggle to understand how practices of civil religion bleed into Christian Nationalism. Some perceive the topic to be primarily about partisan politics rather than a concept identified and rigorously studied by scholars. Education is a powerful tool here. Thankfully, the number of resources to help raise awareness are proliferating.[8] We have cited a number of experts and organizations throughout these chapters. Consider using one of their books or even inviting one of them to speak in

---

[7] A lot of books and resources address how narratives shape churches and stories can be a useful tool for evaluating and enhancing congregational vitality. One foundational example is: James Hopewell, *Congregation: Stories and Structures* (Minneapolis: Fortress Press, 1987).

[8] You're reading this book, after all. We're a little biased, but we think it makes for a great group study or gift for a friend.

your congregation. Promote the event to the public so that others from the community can learn as well. (Perhaps this is the one way Christian Nationalism can help the church: educating others becomes a sneaky evangelism tool!)

An important thing is to not assume people understand Christian Nationalism already. Rather than being frustrated at those who minimize its pernicious effects or fail to grasp what this cultural framework logically entails, commit yourself to studying the topic in depth and invite others to join you. Learn from those who have invested considerable time and energy in explaining it well, especially those doing so because they are concerned about the witness of the Church. You will be better equipped to avoid being complicit in the problem, not to mention countering ignorance or responding to its proponents.

3. Preach a Prophetic Word. After a pastor has learned their respective congregation's story and educated those in their communities, preaching about Christian Nationalism becomes a logical next step. Notice the order here, though. The ground for the sermon should be carefully prepared ahead of time so that the word can actually be heard by the audience. Challenging messages that fall on closed ears do little to change hearts and minds.

The unfortunate reality is that other pulpits serve as platforms for spreading Christian Nationalist ideas. As Rev. Angela Denker, an Evangelical Lutheran Church in America minister, lamented in her book *Red State Christians* after visiting conservative evangelical congregations:

> The near-deification of the American military in many conservative churches is a sign of growing Christian Nationalism and its influence on the local church. ... Support for America as a Christian nation may become the most prominent lesson many American Christians learn in church, rather than a focus on the gospel, on forgiveness, or even on Jesus's death and resurrection.[9]

That's why Randall Balmer, an Episcopal priest and historian of American religion, argued, "We must exorcise the demons of

---

[9] Angela Denker, *Red State Christians: A Journey into White Christian Nationalism and the Wreckage It Leaves Behind* (Minneapolis: Broadleaf Books, 2022), 16–17.

racism and American nationalism. We must step outside of the power structures to recover a prophetic voice. We must look anew at the Scriptures, not as a cudgel to wield against our supposed enemies but as a guide for daily living and a template for how we treat others."[10]

As we see Christian Nationalism's heretical vision for our nation and faith too often proclaimed by preachers and politicians, we recognize that people need to hear the alternative gospel taught in the Bible about Jesus loving the whole world, the reminder that we cannot serve two masters, and the commands for us to love immigrants and even enemies. Preaching about a global faith is perhaps the best way to undermine the theological foundation of Christian Nationalism. It's time for more of us to declare that we're proud Christian globalists! This is the call of God's people at this moment—and always.

We have documented efforts by mainline Protestant preachers to speak out against Christian Nationalism. Some use the Sunday near Flag Day or the Fourth of July as a timely opportunity to offer this timely witness.[11] The need for this kind of approach might be particularly strong in 2026 as the nation celebrates its 250th birthday; the Bicentennial in 1976 resulted in a swell of Christian Nationalism in churches. Other preachers addressing Christian Nationalism focus on liturgical holidays like World Communion Sunday or Christ the King/Reign of Christ Sunday, which have a natural emphasis on how Christianity transcends national boundaries and identity.

"As followers of Jesus Christ, we have to resist Christian Nationalism. There is no room for this idea in the church," Disciples of Christ pastor Tim Trussell-Smith explained in one sermon. "We have to stand up and speak up. We have to tell the truth."[12]

---

[10] Randall Balmer, *Saving Faith: How American Christianity Can Reclaim Its Prophetic Voice* (Minneapolis: Fortress Press, 2023), 75.

[11] Brian Kaylor and Beau Underwood, "Preachers Confront Christian Nationalism," *A Public Witness*, June 13, 2023, https://wordandway. org/2023/06/13/preachers-confront-christian-nationalism.

[12] Brian Kaylor and Beau Underwood, "Preachers United Against Christian Nationalism," *A Public Witness*, October 13, 2022, https:// wordandway.org/2022/10/13/preachers-united-against-christian-nationalism.

"God does not love our country more than others," he added. "We are not supposed to wrap the Bible or God or Jesus up in the flag. And we see that happening. And that is called idolatry."

That message, as they say, will preach.

4. Stop Flying the Flag. Whether outside on a flag pole or in a sanctuary, the U.S. flag remains present in many mainline churches (as well others). It doesn't belong there. The challenge is figuring out how to change the status quo. Many pastors have gotten crossways with their congregations by trying to remove it. Without thinking about the consequences, church members have generated serious conflict in their communities by doing the same.

Hastily disappearing the flag without debate or explanation will likely backfire. It may even become an obstacle to creating an open, constructive conversation within the church that would have been possible before the offense. We would encourage pastors and church members to foster intentional discussions about the flag. Share the history of how it became so common in sanctuaries. Ask people what the flag means to them and why they feel so strongly about its presence in worship (if they do). And invite the congregation to consider what it says about their faith that a national symbol of any country is so prominently displayed in their sacred space.

Anecdotally, this latter point seems most effective in altering the status quo around the flag. A powerful analogy here is the role embassies play in the life of a nation. The United States has outposts in most foreign countries to transact its business. Those embassies enjoy special status and protections despite being on foreign soil. In some respects, you are closer to being in the U.S. than in the host country when you're on the grounds of an embassy. We should see our churches and sanctuaries in the same way. They are outposts of the kingdom of heaven. They should be embassies where people can step out of the world and into an experience of God's realm. There's something different—related to the surrounding environment, but distinctive from it—happening at a church, just like embassies engage with their host countries even as they serve the priorities of their home nation.

Embassies fly the flag of the country they represent, not the country on whose land they sit. Because of their witness to a different kingdom, churches should do the same. The flag of any country does not belong in the embassy of God. We find this metaphor theologically accurate and much more conducive to creating genuine conversations about the appropriateness of flags in churches. It puts the spotlight on the church's true identity rather than on the meaning of Old Glory. It allows Christians to talk about who they are (citizens of the kingdom of God) rather than what they are against (the flag being in the sanctuary).

However you approach the issue, our encouragement is not to remove the flag by fiat. Instead, engage your congregation in conversations about what it means to be Christian, what the flag represents, and what purpose it serves when it's displayed in worship or flies on a pole outside your building. Instead of creating turmoil in your community, there's an opportunity to have an edifying conversation about the Christian life and the problems of Christian Nationalism.

5. Pay Attention to Language and Liturgy. Nations are humanly constructed. Their borders are not divinely ordained. At its most basic level, government is simply how people organize their lives together (fully recognizing that everyone's say in that organization is rarely equal). The foundational myth of Christian Nationalism is that the United States holds a special status in the eyes of God. Language that feeds that narrative by employing religious terms to sacralize the nation and its purposes should be avoided in our churches. Secular holidays that hold little Christian meaning but risk imbuing patriotic occasions with religious meaning should not be observed in our sanctuaries.

The nation should absolutely observe Memorial Day services, but we should not talk about the sacrifices made by soldiers as salvific. We can enjoy the Fourth of July without saying the Pledge of Allegiance or singing the National Anthem in worship (and we'd also advise against lighting off fireworks in your sanctuary). It should be viewed as a national holiday, not a liturgical one. God has entrusted Christ's Church with a powerful story of transcendent love, redemption, and justice. That account of salvation should not be confused or distorted for nationalistic purposes.

Ultimately, Christian Nationalism in our worship services doesn't merely add something that shouldn't be there; it also undermines the very teaching of a God who loves the whole world. As Craig

Watts warned in his book *Bowing Toward Babylon: The Nationalist Subversion of Christian Worship in America*:

> When successfully recruited to serve the nationalistic project, religion can be a powerful tool to deepen national identity, pride, and unity. However, for that to happen the bonds that bind together people of different nations to the same faith must be loosened. Nationalistic worship helps loosen the global unity of Christians. The unity that is reinforced in worship that blends God and nation is the unity of citizens with one another at the expense of the unity of Christians to each other as members of the body of Christ. Nationalism in worship undercuts the unity of Christians given in Jesus Christ through the Holy Spirit.[13]

That's why we warn that Christian Nationalism can become not merely a distortion of our faith but even a competing religion.

6. Urge Institutional Responses and Repentance. This book has highlighted a variety of episodes and ways that mainline Protestants have contributed to the rise and perpetuation of Christian Nationalism. While many mainliners are understandably outraged when other, often more conservative, traditions support this ideology, there has been relatively little attention to this legacy within the mainline denominations. In chapter 2, we highlighted how the 2023 General Assembly of the Christian Church (Disciples of Christ) went on the record opposing Christian Nationalism. Despite the strength of that statement, it still fell critically short: The resolution did not speak to the denomination's past and present involvement in the problem.

Here is a chance to lead by modeling a basic posture of the Christian faith: repentance. Various manifestations of mainline denominations—from the local congregation to the middle adjudicatory (diocese, presbytery, region, conference, etc.) to the denominational heads—should interrogate their pasts, humbly repent of the identified sins, and commit themselves to a more faithful future. Issuing statements of apology and enacting liturgies of confession, making education a priority, and committing to

[13] Craig M. Watts, *Bowing Toward Babylon: The Nationalistic Subversion of Christian Worship in America* (Eugene, OR: Cascade Books, 2017), 9.

disciplines designed to steer clear of Christian Nationalism in their witness are obvious and powerful steps that can be taken at minimal cost. Such efforts enhance integrity and draw attention to the contrast between Christian Nationalism and the gospel proclaimed in Jesus's name.

While not part of a mainline tradition, consider the strong words and actions on this issue from Rev. Matthew Harrison, president of the Lutheran Church-Missouri Synod. In 2023, he published a letter condemning extreme views and hateful rhetoric around race, gender, and other topics that had emerged within the denomination. Some of those espousing the views in the denomination identified as Christian Nationalists, so Harrison demanded repentance from the reprobates and consequences if such contrition was not offered.

"This is evil. We condemn it in the name of Christ," his epistle stated. "Where that call to repentance is not heeded, there must be excommunication."[14]

Harrison's words may sound overly harsh or inappropriate based upon a particular denomination's theology and polity, but the message is quite clear. He defined these positions as outside the bounds of the LCMS and demanded contrition from those advocating for them. His missive received national media attention, thus helping spread the good news about what it means (and does not mean) to follow Jesus.

Expelling Christian Nationalism from American Christianity requires an honest conversation about its reality and humble confession for the mistakes that fueled its rise. Rather than silence or shame, mainline church leaders should recognize the opportunity here to show the world the power of sincere repentance that leads to redemption and results in authentic change.

Onward, Christian People

We anticipate angering a lot of people in writing this book. Those on the far right may dismiss it the way they do other Christian

---

[14] Jack Jenkins and Emily McFarlan Miller, "Lutheran Church-Missouri Synod President Calls for Excommunicating White Nationalists," *Religion News Service*, February 22, 2023, https://religionnews.com/2023/02/22/lutheran-church-missouri-synod-president-calls-for-excommunicating-white-nationalists.

Nationalistic critiques. Other evangelical and conservative Christians may push back on being associated with the criticism directed towards more right-wing segments of American Christianity. And, of course, mainline Protestants—accustomed to denouncing the Christian Nationalism displayed by others—may not enjoy having the light shined on them. Along the way, we have highlighted past missteps by our own denominations, people we admire, and even the publisher of this book. We are not holier than thou. Both of us have been complicit in the problem. We have led and worshiped in churches with flags on the chancel. Even when regularly writing in opposition to Christian Nationalism, we have not always called it out in those places where we have the most influence. As it is with other sins, we are all a work in progress.

Though this book is admittedly contrarian, casting aspersions and fomenting anger is not the goal. As American Christians, we have long belonged to the chorus of voices worried about Christian Nationalism's parasitic relationship with our democracy and our churches. It depends on both institutions to further its goals but damages them along the way. We put pen to paper because we found many people in our professional and church networks were unaware of these stories. They did not understand how "under God" ended up in the Pledge of Allegiance. They had no idea Harry Truman had received the first copy of the Revised Standard Version of the Bible at the White House from leaders of the National Council of Churches. Even where some of the individual episodes had been told, nobody had linked them all together to tell this coherent story. We saw colleagues expressing strong opposition to contemporary expressions of Christian Nationalism without asking how we had collectively reached this point. Caught up in the present moment, they appeared oblivious to their own traditions' past and present contributions to the problem. And, honestly, we learned a lot ourselves. We knew some of the story and went looking for the rest. We found more than we could have imagined (more than could be included in this book). We are certain there's even more we have not yet uncovered.

We want to make a few implications of our argument explicit here at the end. Not only do we believe that the mainline church's role in advancing Christian Nationalism is an overlooked story, but we believe that calling attention to it will lead to positive change. A lot of mainline Protestants remain ignorant of Christian Nationalism's meaning and influence. As this awareness increases, having the courage to interrogate their own congregation and tradition's stories vis-a-vis Christian Nationalism can serve as a catalyst for repentance and correction. Whether due to a lack of awareness, an aversion to introspection, or just plain inertia, we hope this book shifts the debate among mainliners in ways that transform those expressions of Christianity for the better.

As believers in the mainline tradition, this excites us. We hope that wrestling with the issue of Christian Nationalism will refine mainline social witness in ways that gain a new hearing for the gospel. We want these conversations to be formative, allowing mainline Christians to draw closer to Jesus and better understand God's reign. Furthermore, we believe it's time to re-evaluate how Christians in American churches seek to influence public life. Too many remain infatuated with gaining influence and having access to political power. You can explain a lot of the compromises made by churches past and present as an attempt to be—to quote *Hamilton*—"in the room where it happens." Of course, this is generally corrupting. Even politicians and government leaders identifying as Christian rarely adjust their politics based on the demands of their faith, but Christians of all stripes are quick to accommodate. It's easy to see who is leading whom; it's sad to recognize what seems to matter the most. Pastor and theologian Gregory Boyd wrote in *The Myth of a Christian Nation* about this danger:

> The myth of America as a Christian nation, with the church as its guardian, has been, and continues to be, damaging both to the church and to the advancement of God's kingdom. ... This myth harms the church's primary mission. For many in America and around the world, the American flag has smothered the glory of the cross, and the ugliness of our American version of Caesar has squelched the radiant love of Christ. Because the myth that America is a Christian nation has led many to associate America with Christ, many now hear the good news of Jesus only as American news,

capitalistic news, imperialistic news, exploitive news, antigay news, or Republican news.[15]

His words have proved prophetic.

We find Christian Nationalism abhorrent not because we lack appreciation for the privilege of living in the United States and the ideals to which our country aspires but because we are Christians who see its devastating effects on the body of Christ. If we truly believe that Jesus is the Lord of lords and God is sovereign over all the nations, then the ideology of Christian Nationalism must be false. We want to see Christians get their priorities straight. We believe the future of both the Church and the nation depends on it. May God bless not a single country but all of creation. Amen.

---

[15] Gregory A. Boyd, *The Myth of a Christian Nation: How the Quest for Political Power is Destroying the Church* (Grand Rapids: Zondervan, 2005), 13–14.

ACKNOWLEDGEMENTS

One could argue that this book lacks an audience. It critiques mainline Protestants and conservative evangelicals, Republicans and Democrats, past practices and contemporary developments, which begs the question: who will actually enjoy reading it? Despite that dynamic, we believe it covers new and interesting ground in the story it tells and the arguments it makes. We are grateful to Brad Lyons and the team at Chalice Press for taking the risk of putting this out in the world. And we thank all the readers who support Chalice's ministry by choosing to buy the insightful and inspiring books they publish.

We have been writing together for a few years now. People regularly ask about that collaboration. How do we organize who does what? Do we ever disagree? If so, who wins? In truth, we agree on quite a bit and that makes things much easier. We're both committed to a Christian faith that is intellectually engaged and authentically lived. And we're both worried—like many of you—by many of the expressions of Christianity in the U.S. today. We hope our work helps other followers of Jesus to better understand the world and live more faithfully within it. As to our points of disagreement, they're usually over whether our respective jokes are actually funny (but only one of us has actually won awards for humor writing, so that should settle the question).

A couple years ago, we added Jeremy Fuzy into the writing and editorial mix at *Word&Way*. Smart and dedicated in his own right, he has proven immensely valuable in editing our words and ideas in this project. We thank him for the tough questions, keen insights, and encouraging affirmations that improved this book in countless ways. We're glad Chalice brought him into the editing process for this book.

We are also thankful for Rebecca Martin adeptly proofing the book, and for Kesley Houston designing the beautiful cover. Additionally, we are incredibly grateful to Adriene Thorne for her wonderful foreword, and for the other ministers and scholars who read the book and offered their endorsements. It is encouraging and humbling to receive kind words about our work from the likes of Randal Balmer, Jennifer Butler, David Gushee, Bradley Onishi, Paul Brandeis Raushenbush, Jim Wallis, Andrew Whitehead, and Will Willimon.

A few words just from Brian: After a few years of informally solving the world's problems together over chips and salsa during lunches, I eventually convinced Beau to start writing with me at *Word&Way*. I'm still grateful he did. We've had fun and tackled some heavy issues at the intersection of faith and politics that others steer away from (perhaps because they're more concerned about their future employment potential than we are). This book is a longer version of that vision. This project has been a true demonstration of synergy, with it more than twice as good than it would have been if written alone.

I'm also thankful for the support of Jen, who encourages me even when she's not interested in a topic I'm writing about at that moment. She and our son, Kagan, keep me grounded and hopeful even as I venture into odd and dark places for writing topics.

And I'm thankful for the board, readers, donors, and everyone else who supports *Word&Way*. It's an honor to lead this journalism ministry that's been "contending for the word and showing the way" since 1896. I love my job, and so I'm grateful for everyone who makes it possible.

A few words just from Beau: Whenever Brian and I work on a project, I always think of myself as the minor partner. That's true with this book, as he's carried a heavier portion of the load. He has an amazing talent for unearthing interesting data points and connecting them in ways that will make you go, "Ah, now I see it. That's so obvious!" He's one of the smartest Christians I know and works tirelessly on his craft. I've been grateful for him as a boss, colleague, and friend.

I would also use that same phrase—minor partner—to describe my marriage. Casey runs circles around me, and I'm constantly impressed by who she is and all that she does. Her (and our son, Jesse's) constant love and support, especially for my needing to carve out space to write, is incredible. The time away from family is the real opportunity cost of a project like this, which makes every word too expensive.

Finally, I am blessed beyond words to serve as a pastor to those who gather at Allisonville Christian Church (Disciples of Christ) in Indianapolis. They don't bear any responsibility for what we wrote in this book, but I cherish the ways we structure our life together before God. They had already removed all the flags from our sanctuary well before I arrived.

ABOUT THE AUTHORS

Brian Kaylor is a Baptist minister with a Ph.D. in political communication. A former professor of political communication and advocacy studies, he has led *Word&Way* as president and editor-in-chief since 2016. He previously served at churches and denominational organizations affiliated with the Cooperative Baptist Fellowship, American Baptist Churches USA, and Southern Baptist Convention.

Kaylor is the author of multiple books, including *For God's Sake, Shut Up!*, *Presidential Campaign Rhetoric in an Age of Confessional Politics*, and *Sacramental Politics*. An award-winning writer, his pieces have been published by numerous outlets, including *Boston Globe*, CNN, *Houston Chronicle*, *Kansas City Star*, *Nashville Tennessean*, *Sojourners*, and *Washington Post*.

Kaylor serves as board treasurer for Americans United for Separation of Church and State and on the board of the Baptist Peace Fellowship of North America. He also chairs the Resolutions Committee for the Baptist World Alliance.

Beau Underwood is the senior minister of Allisonville Christian Church (Disciples of Christ) in Indianapolis, Indiana. He is also a contributing editor to *Word&Way*. He completed his undergraduate studies at Eureka College, earned graduate degrees in both religion and public policy at the University of Chicago, and is currently pursuing his doctorate in public affairs.

Underwood is the co-author of a book on Christian fatherhood called, *Dear Son: Raising Faithful, Just, and Compassionate Men* that is also published by Chalice Press. His writing has appeared in *Sojourners*, *The Christian Century*, *Religion & Politics*, and other places.

In addition to pastoring and writing, Underwood has worked on political campaigns, progressive faith-based advocacy, and as a hospital chaplain. He has also held a variety of denominational leadership roles, including serving as the 1st vice-moderator of the Christian Church (Disciples of Christ) from 2017-2019.

Word&Way is an independent Christian media outlet that's been faithfully informing since 1896. In addition to a legacy print publication, *Word&Way* also publishes the award-winning e-newsletter *A Public Witness* that provides in-depth reports on faith and politics not found elsewhere. Both Kaylor and Underwood regularly write for *A Public Witness*. Learn more and subscribe at publicwitness.wordandway.org. Additionally, Kayor hosts the *Dangerous Dogma* podcast, and *Word&Way* publishes more news and opinion at wordandway.org.